Strategy Implementation: The Role of Structure and Process

The West Series in Business Policy and Planning

Consulting Editors
Charles W. Hofer
Dan Schendel

Strategy Formulation: Analytical Concepts
Charles W. Hofer and Dan Schendel

Strategy Implementation: The Role of Structure and Process
Jay R. Galbraith and Daniel A. Nathanson

Organizational Goal Structures
Max D. Richards

Strategy Formulation: Political Concepts
Ian C. MacMillan

Strategy Implementation: The Role of Structure and Process

Jay R. Galbraith
Daniel A. Nathanson

The Wharton School
University of Pennsylvania

West Publishing Company
St. Paul   New York   Los Angeles   San Francisco

Library of Congress Cataloging in Publication Data

Galbraith, Jay.
   Strategy implementation.
   (West series in business policy and planning)
   Bibliography: p.
   Includes index.
   1. Organization. 2. Organizational effectiveness. 3. Corporate planning.
I. Nathanson, Daniel A., joint author. II. Title. III. Series.
HD31.G248   658.4'01   78–1849
ISBN 0–8299–0214–7

5th Reprint—1981

To our parents, whose encouragement, guidance, and support have enabled us to grow and to fulfill our potential.

*

Contents

*

Foreword

The purpose of this common foreword to all the volumes in the *West Series on Business Policy and Planning* is threefold: first, to provide background to the reader on the origins and purposes of the series; second, to describe the overall design of the series and the contents of the texts contained in the series; and third, to describe ways in which the series or the individual texts within it can be used.

This series is a response to the rapid and significant changes that have occurred in the policy area over the past fifteen years. While business policy is a subject of long standing in management schools, it has traditionally been viewed as a capstone course whose primary purpose was to *integrate* the knowledge and skills students had gained in the functional disciplines. During the past decade, however, policy has developed a substantive content of its own that has permitted it to emerge as a discipline in its own right. Originally, this content focused on the concept of organizational strategy and on the processes by which such strategies were formulated and implemented within organizations. More recently, the scope of the field has broadened to include the study of all the functions and responsibilities of top management, together with the organizational processes and systems for formulating and implementing organizational strategy. To date, however, this extension in scope has not been reflected in texts in the field.

The basic purpose of the *West Series on Business Policy and Planning* is to fill this void through the development of a series of texts that cover the policy field while incorporating the latest research findings and conceptual thought.

In designing the series, we took care to ensure, not only that the various texts fit together as a series, but also that each text is self-contained and addresses a major topic in the field. In addition, each text is written so that it can be used at both the advanced undergraduate and the masters level. The first four texts, which cover topics in the heart of the policy field, are:

Organizational Goal Structures, by Max D. Richards.

Strategy Formulation: Analytical Concepts, by Charles W. Hofer and Dan Schendel.

Strategy Formulation: Political Concepts, by Ian C. MacMillan.

Strategy Implementation: The Role of Structure and Process, by Jay R. Galbraith and Daniel A. Nathanson.

A second set of texts are in preparation and should be available next year. They will cover additional topics in policy and planning such as the behavioral and social systems aspects of the strategy formulation process, environment forecasting, strategic control, formal planning systems, and the strategic management of new ventures. Additional texts covering still other topics are being considered for the years following.

The entire series has been designed so that the texts within it can be used in several ways. First, the individual texts can be used to supplement the conceptual materials contained in existing texts and case books in the field. In this regard, explicit definitions are given for those terms and concepts for which there is as yet no common usage in the field, and, whenever feasible, the differences between these definitions and those in the major texts and case books are noted. Second, one or more of the series texts can be combined with cases drawn from the Intercollegiate Case Clearing House to create a hand-crafted case course suited to local needs. To assist those interested in such usage, most texts in the series include a list of ICCH cases that could be used in conjunction with it. Finally, the series can be used without other materials by those who wish to teach a theory-oriented policy course. Thus, the series offers the individual instructor flexibility in designing a policy course. Finally, because of their self-contained nature, each of the texts can also be used as a supplement to various nonpolicy courses within business and management school curricula.

Charles W. Hofer

Dan Schendel

Consulting Editors

September, 1977

Preface

This book attempts to deal with issues of design of the overall organization structure. As such, it carries on the tradition of Alfred Chandler's *Strategy and Structure*, which proposes that the structure of the organization should be linked to the product-market strategy pursued by the firm. In this book we try to show how variation in organization structure and process should be matched with variation in strategy. Our work is based upon the empirical and theoretical studies that have been triggered by Chandler's study and, as such, represents a review of the Business Policy and Organization Theory literature. We have searched for those empirical studies that link strategy, structure, process, and performance, which are reviewed to see what we know about the strategy-structure linkage.

Our treatment departs from other works as well as from Chandler's, in that we have tried explicitly to expand the notion of organization to include more than just departmental structure and the degree of centralization. We have tried to focus also upon the process of integrating departments, resource allocation processes, reward systems and people. There has not been a great deal of research concerning relationships among these variables, but we have reviewed the studies that have been performed. Some cases are given as examples to fill in the gaps.

Our basic premise is that effective financial performance is obtained by the achievement of congruence between strategy, structure, processes, rewards, and people. This is an equilibrium-like state that is never achieved but always sought. The move from one strategy to another requires a disengaging, realignment, and a reconnecting of all these factors. In this book we discuss the different types of organizational forms that can result from such efforts. We do not talk of the problem of managing the transition from one form to another. Instead, we concentrate upon the conditions under which one form would be preferable to another.

In addition to reviewing the state-of-the-art of our knowledge about strategy and structure, we also look at those organizations that are inventing the new structures of today. Chandler focussed upon General Motors and DuPont as they were organized in the 1920s, when they invented the multi-divisional form. We ask whether there is a new form being invented now, and discuss the evolving matrix organization forms, the strategic business unit (SBU's) planning structures, and Office of the President concepts. Many of the organizations using these forms are pursuing strategies of multiple sources of diversity. They are large multi-product, multi-market and multi-national firms.

This book, which is intended as a text for advanced undergraduate and MBA policy courses, also provides recommended cases to go with selected chapters. A second audience for the book is the organization designer. Some of the literature reviewed here is unknown to organization theorists, because it comes from the field of Business Policy. Other work is unknown to Business Policy scholars because it is buried in the organization literature. Because our focus is upon the organization we may have missed some policy works. Our intention, however was to bring the two fields together in considering the choice of the organization structure for strategy implementation. Hence the audience is the organization designer, whether academic or manager, rather than the organization theorist.

We would like to thank several people for their help in preparing this book. First, Chuck Hofer helped considerably with his line by line review and made many suggestions which improved the manuscript. We also want to thank Cindi Kee and Sue Shaw for typing the manuscript under our rushed schedule. They are most patient and understanding in dealing with our frantic last minute deadlines. In addition, we would like to express our appreciation to the management of Vernitron Corporation for making a commitment to this work and for having the foresight to realize the importance and potential long-run benefits of the academic experience. Finally we want to thank our families for their continuous support during our ups and downs.

†

1

Introduction

This chapter presents an overview of the book by introducing an overall framework, along with some important concepts and key definitions.

The basic premise with which we begin is that an organization has a variety of structural forms and organizational processes to choose from when implementing a chosen strategy. It is our contention that the choice of structural forms makes an economic difference; that is, all structural forms are not equally effective in implementing a given strategy. Therefore, organization members should allocate the time and effort necessary to plan their organizational form, just as time and effort are allocated for the formulation of other plans.

There are, however, other design variables in addition to structure to be considered if a firm is to marshal its resources effectively and implement its strategy. The organization must be designed to facilitate the proper selection, training, and development of its people. They must be able to perform their tasks and thereby carry out the desired strategy. Congruent reward systems must provide the incentives necessary for people to work effectively and in harmony with the organization's goals. Information must also be available to control and coordinate activities, to measure performance effectively, and to monitor and plan. Hence, the choice of organization form consists of a comprehensive design of structure, systems, and processes.

The major design variables that will be presented in this book are represented schematically below:

Figure 1.1 Schematic Showing Fit Among Major Organization Design Variables

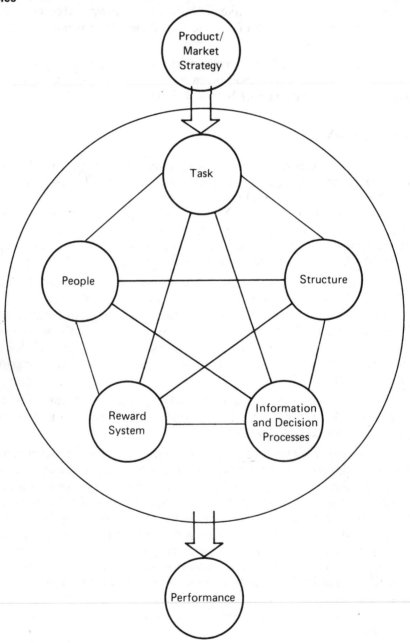

Each of these variables represents a choice for the organization. However, to be successful, the choices should be internally consistent and also consistent with the firm's product-market strategy. Generally, it has been found that structural choice follows from strategic choice. The decision to make a change in strategy often calls for a change in the entire set of design variables. The process is one of constant readjustment.

We have mentioned the terms *strategy, structure,* and *process.* It is essential that we now look more precisely at these terms before we delve into the relationships between them.

DEFINITIONS

The word *strategy,* which derives from the ancient Greek word *strategos,* meaning "the art of the general", has since taken on a variety of broad and often ambiguous definitions. For instance, in game theory, strategy is concerned principally with a statistical set of rules for the player to improve the probabilities of a desired payoff. In this book, however, we are concerned with strategy as specific actions deriving from the "strategy formulation process."

Strategy formulation has itself been defined in a variety of ways. Hofer and Schendel view strategy formulation as the process of deciding the basic mission of the company, the objectives that the company seeks to achieve, and the major strategies and policies governing the use of the firm's resources to achieve its objectives (Hofer and Schendel 1978). The interested reader should see their companion volume in this series.

Strategy, then, means a specific action, usually but not always accompanied by the development of resources, to achieve an objective decided upon in strategic planning.

It becomes apparent that if a strategy is a specific action, then many *strategies* can be identified in large-scale organizations. Alfred D. Chandler in his book *Strategy and Structure* (1962) distinguished certain key growth strategies that were most important for insuring the long-term survival of the organization. The strategies identified were expansion of volume, geographic dispersion, vertical integration, and product diversification. Chandler showed how each strategy posed a different type of administrative difficulty and, therefore, tended to lead to a different form of organizational structure. Many theorists in various disciplines have dealt with these same strategies and with the same basic issue of the strategy-structure "fit" shown in Figure 1.2.

Figure 1.2

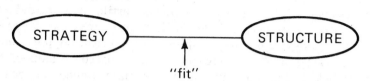

"fit"

This book reviews the work of Chandler and of theorists in areas such as economics, sociology, business policy, and organization behavior. Although the vocabulary of each field differs somewhat, many similarities between them can be pinpointed.

The first growth strategy that Chandler discussed, expansion of volume, refers to increased sales in a single market or in existing markets, whereas geographical diversification (the second strategy) is the entry into geographically different markets. Vertical integration represents the third growth strategy and is characterized by the firm's absorption of its suppliers or industrial customers. Therefore, the major activities of these vertically integrated companies usually consist of stages in the sequential processing of a particular material from its raw form to a finished product (Scott 1967; Remelt 1974). A simplified diagram of a vertically integrated oil company is shown in Figure 1.3.

Figure 1.3

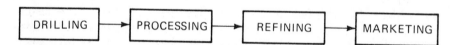

The strategies of product and market diversification represent the major direction of research and attention in this book. As will be shown, product diversified firms have become the dominant type of organization, not only in the U.S. but also abroad. Chandler defines diversification as the development of new products. Subsequently other theorists such as Leonard Wrigley (1970) and Richard Rumelt (1974) refined the concept by classifying four types of diversification. These are single product business, dominant business, related product business, and unrelated product business. Wrigley's diversification classification begins with the *single product business*, which includes firms such as Maytag, makers of washing machines and dryers; Wrigley, the chewing gum manufacturers; and Schlitz and Falstaff, brewers. The next category is *the dominant business*, in which one product accounts for 70 to 95 percent of the firm's total sales. Examples include most of the oil companies: Mobil, Gulf, Atlantic Richfield, and Continental, to name a few. Their dominant product, of course, is oil, but they have diversified vertically and into businesses such as plastics, petrochemicals, fertilizers, coal, and atomic energy. Other examples include Philip Morris, who has added beer, gum, razor blades, toiletries, hospital and surgical supplies, etc., to their dominant business of cigarettes and tobacco. Campbell Soup has added baked goods and candy to its dominant canned soup business. *The related product business* represents the third category. Firms in this category have diversified more than 30 percent of their sales outside their main business, but they have done so by selling products related by either common customer, common distribution channels, technology, etc. That is, some connection existed between the products. An example is Dow-Corning, which diversified its product line but remained with products that used silicon technology. Other examples include Du Pont, General Electric, General Foods, General Mills, Gillette, Johnson and Johnson, Proctor and Gamble, and Westinghouse. The final category is the *unrelated business* organization. Here the firms have more than 30 percent of their sales outside their main business, but these other businesses have little or no relation to each other. Examples of such firms include Colt Industries, Curtiss-Wright, FMC, Litton Industries, and Rockwell Manufacturing. These different types of diversification strategies have been shown to have different effects on organization structure and process. — *Rumelt*

What, then, is meant by the terms *structure* and *process*? Chandler defines structure (1962, p. 14) as the design of organization through which the enterprise is administered. He goes on to state, "the design, whether formally or informally defined has two aspects, first the lines of authority and communication between the different administrative offices and officers and second the information and data that flow through these lines of communication and authority." Organization theorists such as John Child (1972) define structure as the formal allocation of work roles and the administrative mechanisms to control and integrate work activity, including those that cross formal organizational boundaries. We view structure as the segmentation of work into roles such as production, finance, marketing, and so on; the recombining of roles into departments or divisions around functions, products, regions, or markets; and the distribution of power across this role structure. We view processes as the direction and frequency of work and information flows linking the differentiated roles within and between departments of the complex organization.

There are several structural types, including the centralized functional organization, the decentralized multi-divisional form, the holding company form, and the newer matrix form. A centralized organization is characterized by the locus of power concentrated at the top of the organization.   Conversely, a decentralized organization is one in which power and decision making authority are found at lower levels in the organization.   The functional organization is usually more centralized, and its departments are specialized and arranged by function, such as marketing, finance, manufacturing, and legal.   Organization charts representing the functional, multi-divisional, holding company, and matrix structures are shown in Figures 1.4 through 1.7 respectively.

The multi-divisional organization is generally more decentralized than the functional organization, because the departments are separated on the basis of product, market, or region.   Usually all the resources necessary to manufacture and sell the product or to supply the market are put under the control of a particular division.   The division manager, therefore, is given considerable authority and responsibility. The holding company form is one in which even greater authority and responsibility are given to the divisions.   The corporate office is smaller than that of the multi-divisional firm because the corporate office merely performs the function of capital allocation.   Finally, the matrix organization, represented in Figure 1.7, reflects both a function and a product orientation.   Many variations to the structures mentioned above exist and will be discussed.   This presentation was made merely to introduce the concepts in an understandable fashion.

Now that we have defined the terms *strategy*, *structure*, and *process*, albeit briefly, we are able to introduce some of the major concepts, issues, hypotheses, and theories that are presented in this book.

CONCEPTS, ISSUES, HYPOTHESES AND THEORIES

Chandler's general thesis is that structure follows strategy.   Changes in a firm's strategy result from an awareness of the opportunities and needs—created by changing population, income, and technology— to employ existing or expanding resources more profitably.   The new strategy brings about new administrative problems, however.   These new administrative problems require a new or, at least, a refashioned structure if the enlarged enterprise is to operate efficiently.

Our examples above illustrate some of the main strategy-structure relationships.   Basically, the firms with single and dominant product strategies utilize the functional form illustrated by the dictaphone corporation in Figure 1.4.   Similarly, most business related firms such as Texas Instruments have a multi-divisional structure.   Finally,

Figure 1.4 A Functional Organization (The Dictaphone Corporation)

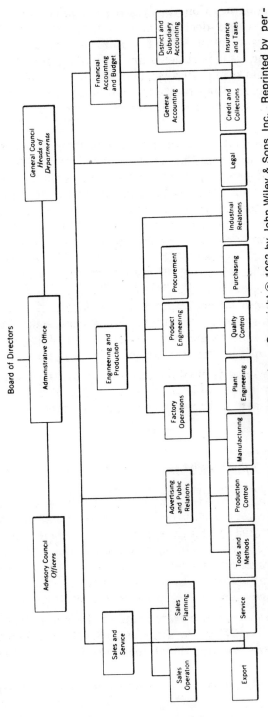

From Joseph A. Litterer, *Organizations: Structure and Behavior.* Copyright © 1963 by John Wiley & Sons, Inc. Reprinted by permission of John Wiley & Sons, Inc.

Figure 1.5 A Multi-Divisional Structure at Texas Instruments

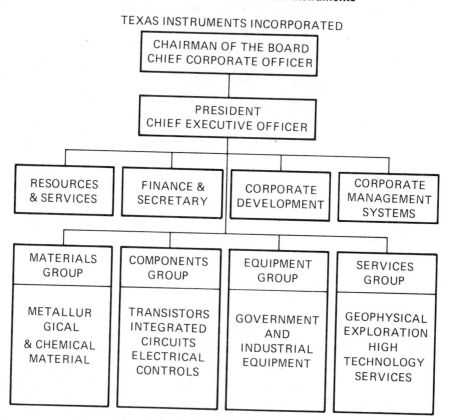

This figure appears in the case 9–672–036. Copyright © 1971 by the President and Fellows of Harvard College. Reproduced by permission.

Figure 1.6 Hypothetic Unrelated Business Corporation

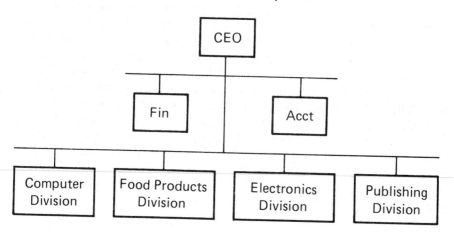

Figure 1.7 The Dow-Corning Matrix (1973)

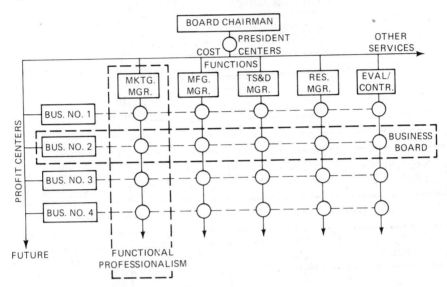

most unrelated product firms generally use the holding company form. Therefore, as we move from the single product firm to the unrelated firm, we also see a move from centralization to decentralization. The greater decentralization is presumably needed to cope with the additional uncertainty and diversity presented by the firm's product-market strategy.

Chandler's thesis, then, represents what is currently known in the organization field as a contingency theory. Contingency theory states there is no one best way to organize, but that all ways of organizing are not equally effective (Galbraith 1973). The choice is dependent or contingent upon something. Chandler suggests that structure is contingent upon the growth strategy. Subsequent theorists have elaborated upon this idea and added some other contingencies. Thus, the greater the diversity among products or markets or both, the greater the likelihood that the successful organization will be multi-divisional, as opposed to functional. Moreover, with greater diversity, decision-making power for operations is more likely to be concentrated at lower levels in the successful organization. The research and analysis supporting these statements are presented in the next three chapters.

The design of the organization is more than a choice of alternative divisional structures. This point is illustrated in Figure 1.1, where structure is but one dimension of the organization form that intervenes between strategy and performance. However, other dimensions such as resource allocation processes, information systems, cross-departmental decision processes, career paths, and compensation systems have not received the same level of research attention that has been accorded to structure. They have received attention, but there has been little attempt to match variations in these systems and processes with variations in strategy and performance. Therefore, the smaller amount of attention given them reflects only the research that has been conducted, not the intrinsic importance of these dimensions. In any case, our belief is that variation in strategy should be matched with variation in processes and systems as well as in structure, in order for organizations to implement strategies successfully. The specific ways in which dimensions should vary are described in chapters five and six.

The key concept and hypothesis that we would like to present is that of consistency or fit and its relation to effectiveness. That is, the design problem is more than one of matching strategy and structure and matching processes and strategy. It requires matching all these dimensions to one another as well as to strategy, in order to achieve a fit, a consistency, or a congruence among all organization dimensions. We regard the achievement of fit as the most important feature of an organizational contribution to economic effectiveness. This concept is dealt with in more detail in chapter seven.

As a consequence of the relation between consistency and performance, the design and redesign of organizations is a massive undertaking requiring substantial time and effort. Therefore, each major change has been hypothesized as constituting a different stage of organization development. Several authors as well as Chandler have proposed such stagewise growth models to explain the development of American corporate structures. These models are reviewed and analyzed in chapter eight.

Questions naturally emerge from the discussion of stages of growth. Are we in a new stage now? Is the matrix a new stage of corporate development? The current state-of-the-art in organizational structure and process is analyzed from this perspective in chapter nine. These new structures are described and analyzed from the point of view of consistency between strategy and structure.

SUMMARY

This chapter introduces the major concepts to be used in this book in order to provide a way of talking about strategy and structure. Strategy was defined, and four specific types of strategy were identified. Four alternative structures were also enumerated, together with various organizational processes. The main emphasis was that the organization must achieve a fit between its strategy, its structure, and its processes. The achievement of this fit, or the lack thereof, is hypothesized as having an economic impact that is crucial, especially in the presence of competition. These ideas are elaborated in subsequent chapters. The next chapter, chapter two, deals with the "Conceptual Foundations of Strategy and Structure." It lays the groundwork for the "Empirical Foundations" which follow in chapter three.

2

Conceptual Foundations
of Strategy and Structure

In this chapter, the conceptual foundations of the strategy-structure linkage are presented by reviewing the works of Chandler, Williamson, and Thompson. Chandler's historical study *Strategy and Structure* has stimulated conceptual and empirical works of an interdisciplinary nature. Williamson, an economist, discusses the divisionalized firm and its ability to internalize the market mechanism. Thompson, a sociologist, views the organization-environment interaction in terms of interdependencies and domains. Although the vocabularies of various disciplines appear different, there appears to be a surprising consistency of concepts among them. All three theorists help explain why strategy and structure are related and also provide insight into the growth of organizations.

CHANDLER'S THESIS

The recent scholarly interest in strategy and structure connections outside of business policy textbooks was impelled by the publication of Chandler's research in *Strategy and Structure* (Chandler 1962). On the basis of a historical study of seventy of America's largest firms, he formulated several hypotheses that stimulated much of the subsequent work. First, he proposed the principle that organization structure follows the growth strategy of the firm. Second, he proposed a stagewise developmental sequence for the strategies and structures of American enterprises. Third, he theorized that organizations do not change their structures until they are provoked by inefficiency to do so. In part, this is because the formulator of strategies is rarely the creator of organizations. Let us look briefly at each of these points prior to reviewing the studies that followed from them.

Chandler's work is best known for the hypothesis that is suggested in the title of his book. "The thesis deduced from these several propositions is then that structure follows strategy and that the most complex type of structure is the result of the concatenation of several basic strategies." (Chandler 1962, p. 14). Thus, the structure of an organization follows from its growth strategy. Specifically, as organizations change their growth strategy in order to employ resources more profitably in the face of changing technology, income, and population, the new strategy poses new administrative problems. These administrative problems are solved only by refashioning the organization structure to fit the new strategy. A corollary to this thesis is that if a structural adjustment does not take place, the strategy will not be completely effective, and economic inefficiency will result. Chandler proposed a sequence consisting of new strategy creation, emergence of new administrative problems, decline in economic performance, invention of a new appropriate structure, and subsequent recovery to profitable levels.

In his historical study, the above sequence was seen to be repeated often as American firms grew and changed their growth strategies. Initially, most firms were units such as plants, sales offices, or warehouses in a single industry, a single location, and a single function of either manufacturing, sales, or wholesaling. Initial growth was simply *volume expansion,* but it created a need for an administrative office. Next, a *geographic expansion* strategy created multiple field units in the same function and industry but in different locations. Administrative problems of interunit coordination, specialization, and standardization arose, and the functional departmental office was created to handle these issues. During the 1800s, these issues were first confronted by the railroads, which were the innovators emulated by other industries. Today, the same issues are raised by branch banking. Figure 2.1 shows the strategies and the resulting structures that evolved.

The next stage in the historical development of growth consisted of the strategies that involved *vertical integration.* That is, successful business firms stayed in the same industry but acquired or cre-

Figure 2.1 Strategies and Structure

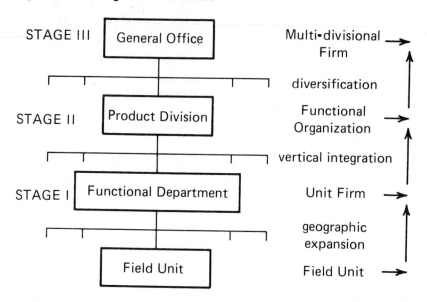

ated other functions. Manufacturing plants created their own ware-houses and wholesaling operations and their own sales force. New administrative problems arose in the effort to balance the sequential movement of goods through the interdependent functions. This led to the development of forecasts, schedules, and capacity balancing techniques. Here the innovators were the steel companies that integrated back to the mining operations.

The last strategy analyzed by Chandler was the one of *product diversification*. Firms moved into new industries in order to employ existing resources as primary markets declined. The new problems in this case centered on the appraisal and evaluation of product divisions and alternative investment proposals. Time had to be allowed for the strategic management of this capital allocation process. The multi-divisional structure shown in Figure 2.1 was the new form of organization that evolved. This form, which created a division of labor based on a time horizon, was superior to the functional organization as a means of managing capital allocation in the face of diversity. The divisions were responsible for short-run operating decisions; the central office was responsible for strategic, long-run decisions. The office was to be staffed with general managers who were not responsible for short-run operating results and were there-by given the time and psychological commitment necessary for long-term planning in the interest of the corporation as a whole. There were enough general managers, usually group executives, to tie that strategic direction to internal control of divisional performance. However, there was not excessive management which often led to local interference. In this way, the divisional form was superior to the functional organization and the holding company.

The first companies to create the multi-divisional form were those that first experienced the effects of diversity. Du Pont and General Motors were the innovators this time. Their stories and those of Sears Roebuck and Standard Oil make up the bulk of Chandler's book. He then traces the development of this new form throughout American enterprise. However, not all of the firms adopted the multi-divisional form. The copper and aluminum companies, for example, did not. These were the companies that did not diversify product lines, however; they grew in one industry and supplied the same customers, employing strategies mentioned above as those of single and dominant product businesses. Thus, these firms also demonstrate that structure follows strategy. Those firms that remained and grew within a single industry retained the centralized functional organization; those that diversified adopted the multi-divisional structure. This strategy-structure linkage has been the part of Chandler's work that has been examined and reformulated most in subsequent studies. It is not his only point, however.

A second part of Chandler's thesis is the hypothesis concerning the stagewise development of American enterprise.

> Thus four phases of chapters can be discerned in the history of the large American industrial enterprise: the initial expansion and accumulation of resources; the rationalization of the use of resources; the expansion into new markets and lines to help assure the continuing full use of resources; and finally the development of a new structure to make possible continuing effective mobilization of resources to meet both changing short-term market demands and long-term market trends. (Chandler 1962, p. 385).

Thus, we have a strategy of resource accumulation followed by a rationalization of its use through the functional organization structure. Next came expansion into new markets through diversification, followed by the creation of the multi-divisional structure in order to achieve a division of labor based on a time horizon. Figure 1.1 represents these changes as changes from Stage I through Stage III, to use the terms applied by Scott in subsequent works (Scott 1967, 1973). As Stage I organizations accumulated resources through vertical integration, they changed structures to the Stage II functional structure. After changing strategy to one of diversification, they changed structure again to the Stage III multi-divisional form. This sequence was proposed as the stagewise development model of American enterprise. This model too has stimulated a good deal of subsequent study.

Although the last point to be discussed has not stimulated much subsequent empirical inquiry, it is becoming entrenched in current practice. Chandler found that the empire builder or the strategy formulator was rarely the individual who created the new structure to fit the new strategy. Those who acquired resources had professional backgrounds and interests different from those of the organizational innovators. One result of these divergent modes of training and thought was that the entrepreneur rarely took time to do the logical thinking necessary for organizational analysis. As a result, the move from one stage of structure to another was a painful one. It was only when economic inefficiency resulted and an entrepreneur left that the new structure was created and put into place. Thus, the psychological difference between the entrepreneur and the organizer caused a delay between the formulation of strategy and implementation of structure and the implementation of a new structure occurred only after severe provocation.

In summary, three main principles can be identified in Chandler's work.

—Organization structure follows from the growth strategy pursued by the firm.

—American firms have followed a pattern of stagewise development from unifunctional structure, to the functional organization, to the multi-divisional structure.

—The change from one stage to another occurred only after provocation, because the strategy formulator and the organizational innovator were different types of people.

In the following chapters of this book, these points will be reviewed together with empirical evidence created by subsequent research. The next section examines the first and primary thesis, that structure follows strategy.

STRATEGY AND STRUCTURE

The idea that strategy and structure are closely linked was picked up quickly by a number of different disciplines. In business schools, the business policy, organization behavior, and management groups all incorporated it into their literature. Most empirical work has come from these sources. In addition, economists and sociologists with an interest in organization theory have adopted it to confirm some of their ideas, making some conceptual elaborations and extensions of the concepts. Let us begin with this latter group before reviewing the empirical work.

MARKETS AND HIERARCHIES: AN ECONOMIC PERSPECTIVE

The most extensive study of structure that has been made by an economist is that of Oliver Williamson (1970, 1975). Williamson is a leading theorist in the new field of institutional economics, which developed methods of analyzing microeconomic phenomena in a more detailed yet rigorous manner. The primary focus of such research is on the cost of transactions. This focus leads Williamson and others to examine different institutional arrangements for conducting economic activity. In the past, economists have been primarily preoccupied with prices and markets as the only institutions through which efficient economic transactions could take place. The institutionalists, however, see markets and firms as alternative institutions through which to conduct economic transactions. Society should then choose the form that is more efficient or provides the lesser cost vehicle for the conduct of economic activity.

Williamson makes an argument that is obvious to business policy and organization theorists but not necessarily to economists: internal organization makes an economic difference. Therefore, economists should be as concerned with internal organization structure as they are with market structure. Specifically, he suggests that when there are exchange circumstances characterized by uncertainty, and by idiosyncratic knowledge, small numbers, and opportunistic behavior, then market prices and market substitutes such as contracting are inefficient or unfair. Instead, it is more efficient to use an administrative process which takes an adaptive approach to uncertainty by making a sequence of decisions and transmitting the newly acquired information between the interested parties. He suggests that internal organization and administrative processes as we know them are the result of the forementioned market failures. That is, under circumstances of uncertainty, of differentially distributed information, of opportunism, and of small numbers of participants, the invisible hand fails to do its job of clearing markets in an economically efficient manner. An inventor of an institutional form to replace the defective market can reap the benefits of increased economic efficiency. Such is the case with vertically integrated work flows managed through functional organizations instead of bilateral monopoly bargaining. Such is also the case with diversified businesses managed through the multi-divisional structure, rather than by a capital market allocating funds to functional organizations.

Williamson's view of the multi-divisional firm as a miniature capital market is an interesting one. He sees the multi-divisional form as a response to the inability of both functional organizations and capital markets to regulate decision making discretion in organizations following both a substantial separation of management and ownership and an increase in a firm's size and complexity.

> A search for substitute *external* controls has been set in motion on this account: solemn supplications on behalf of corporate responsibility have also been advanced. But the possibility that discretionary outcomes might be checked by *reorganizational* changes within the firm has been generally neglected. I submit, however, that organization innovations, which in the 1930s were just getting underway, have mitigated capital market failures by transferring functions traditionally imputed to the capital market to the firm instead. Not only were the direct effects of substituting internal organization for the capital market beneficial, but the indirect effects served to renew the efficacy of capital market controls as well. (Williamson 1975, p. 136).

Williamson argues that for large firms operating in diverse businesses, the multi-divisional structure is a more effective means of allocating capital in order to maximize profit than either the functional organization, the holding company, or businesses operating as independent units regulated only by product and capital markets. The argument proposed here against the functional organization is similar to Chandler's and Berg's empirical work (Berg 1965). As a result of an insufficient number of general managers, the organization is unable to separate short-term operating decisions from long-term strategic decisions. The divisional form produces optimal allocation more often than individual units operating independently, because the incentive machinery of the organization creates greater goal compatibility between divisions and management than that existing between owners and managers. In addition, management is

better informed than investors because of information systems and
more thorough audits, and because they allocate capital across divisions from low to high yield divisions with less cost than the capital
market. The divisional form is superior to the holding company as
well. Although the holding company can allocate cash flows from
low to high yield division, it lacks the information and management
necessary for strategic planning and internal control. In fact, the
holding company is viewed as being little different from the capital
market.

Thus, for diversified businesses, the economic performance of the
multi-divisional form usually is higher than that of the functional
organization, the holding company, and the operation of the divisions
as independent companies. The comparison with holding companies
is useful because it demonstrates that merely converting to a divisional form is not enough. Conversion must be accompanied by
strategic direction, by internal incentives and controls, and by a
management style that delegates short-run operation to the divisions.
This package of structure, strategy, and process is a concept to which
we shall return. Thus, the theoretical dimension of Williamson's
work permits greater rigorous analyses of the implications of
Chandler's initial findings.

DOMAIN AND STRUCTURE:
A SOCIOLOGICAL PERSPECTIVE

A second conceptual framework comes from James D. Thompson,
a sociologist, whose distinctive approach is nonetheless very similar
to Williamson's, because it also studies uncertainty, diversity, and
bounded rationality (Thompson 1967, Chapters 3 to 6). Thompson's
interpretation provides the most complete statement of how organizations both shape and are shaped by their environments, because
his propositions relate to choices of strategy as well as to those of
structure. His arguments are summarized briefly here; the unfamiliar reader is advised to refer to the original and to Galbraith's
elaboration (Galbraith 1977, Chapters 13 and 14).

Thompson begins his analysis of organization-environment interaction with the proposition that organizations stake out domains;
that is, they make claims that they will offer certain products or
services to certain customers or clients. In the terminology of business policy, this is simply the firm's product-market strategy. The
term *domain* is used in organizational sociology to denote a generalization to all types of organizations. The significance of the choice

of domain or product-market strategy is that, together with the choice of technology, it determines the points at which the organization is dependent upon others for the resources, referrals, and other types of support required for its survival. Choices of domain reduce the environment from an amorphous "everything else" to a specific group of suppliers, users, competitors, and regulatory agencies upon which the focal organization is dependent. The cooperation of this set of environmental groups is required for viability.

Domains are not unilaterally determined, however. Given scarcity of resources and competitors for domains, environmental support must be earned and sustained. A domain becomes operational only when the organization's rights to domain are recognized by those whose support is needed. Once the expectations of the environmental groups on which the organization is dependent have been met, a concensus concerning domain exists. The concept of domain concensus is similar to the business policy concept of product-market distinctive competence. The difference appears to be that distinctive competence is defined from the point of view of the focal organization, and domain consensus is defined from the point of view of environmental groups. Thus far, there has been little cross-fertilization between the groups using these separate but similar terms.

The next step in Thompson's scheme is to recognize that domain consensus must be maintained continually in the context of changing technology, population, and competition. Given change and dependency on others, Thompson expects organizations to manage these dependency relations by trading on the dependencies of other organizations in the environment. This view causes him to focus on power-dependence relations among organizations.

Thompson's descriptive propositions concerning environmental management differ from the normative strategy literature at this point, but they are nonetheless very relevant to it. (Many expansions of these ideas are presented in MacMillan's companion volume in this series (MacMillan 1978)). Thompson's view is very close to Williamson's. In managing power-dependence relations, organizations promote distinctive competence when faced with large numbers of suppliers and users. This is the competitive response, and theories of prices and markets apply. However, when suppliers and users become concentrated (Williamson's small numbers condition), the organization seeks to gain power relative to those sources upon which it depends by exploiting their own dependency. He develops a number of propositions about how organizations defend their domains and analyzes the conditions under which they will reduce the uncertainty surrounding their dependency by means of contracting, and by either co-opting dependent elements or coalescing with them through joint ventures. Each of these cooperative moves reduces uncertainty about the continued support from sources on which the organization is dependent and thus guarantees viability.

The defense of domains can become costly, however. Contracting reduces flexibility to act over the length of the agreement; co-optation enters an external element, such as a banker, directly into the organization's decision process; and joint ventures reduce flexibility even more by forcing two sovereign organizations to act as one. If an organization has strong technological dependencies and is operating under unstable conditions, continued support from the environment becomes a serious problem. It requires finding and holding a position that is recognized by all environmental groups as more worthwhile than other alternatives. One would expect, therefore, that organizations would minimize the need for this environmental maneuvering by incorporating critical dependencies within the boundaries of the organization.

Thompson poses a number of hypotheses that predict the direction in which an organization will grow on the basis of its critical dependence upon an environmental component. He uses much of Chandler's work as data to support the growth strategy propositions, employing the concept of interdependence to distinguish between different kinds of dependencies. Figure 2.2 shows the three different kinds of interdependencies.

Figure 2.2: Types of Interdependence

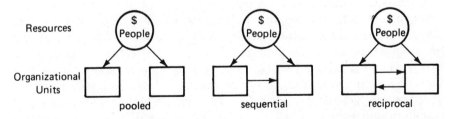

The simplest type of interdependence is pooled. It simply means that two units share the same pool of resources such as money, managerial talent, or space. The second type is sequential interdependence, where there is a movement of work between units, as in a fabricating and assembly operation. Sequential interdependence is more critical than pooled, because sequentially interdependent units have pooled linkages in addition to the sequential. The third and most critical type of interdependence is reciprocal. An example of this is an assembly unit that feeds an inspection operation that in turn feeds back the pieces to the assembly unit. If two units have reciprocal interdependence, then they also have sequential and pooled interdependencies. Each one represents increasing costs of coordination, pooled being the least costly and reciprocal the most. From these types of interdependencies, Thompson explains why organizations grew and structured their operations in the stages that Chandler observed.

Organizations are predicted to grow by incorporating within their boundaries those elements that, if left outside, would pose critical contingencies for viability and be costly to manage by contracting. Elements exhibiting reciprocal interdependence would be the first ones acquired by the organization or created within its boundaries. Initially, growth involved acquisition of the full complement of functional elements to form the Stage I unifunctional unit. The next stage of growth was vertical integration, or the incorporation of sequentially interdependent elements. The result was the Stage II functional organization. Then, excess capacity in the high investment of crucial functions led to diversification into new domains that shared the underutilized technology. In short, diversification created pooled interdependence among units sharing the common technology or distribution channel and, thereby, the Stage III firm.

The strategies led to different structures. Again, interdependence was the primary determinant of structure. First, organizations group in common units all elements that are reciprocally interdependent, in order to minimize coordination costs. After reciprocally interdependent elements have been grouped, all sequentially interdependent elements are grouped in common units. Finally, all pooled elements are brought together. However, not all elements can be placed in a single cluster to be coordinated by a single manager. Therefore, the concept of hierarchy, shown in Figure 1.3, must be introduced. At the first level, all reciprocally interdependent elements are grouped until they exceed the span of control of the manager. Then, a second level grouping is used to exhaust the remaining reciprocally interdependent units. If none are remaining, the sequentially interdependent elements are grouped into a second-order cluster. Finally, pooled elements form the final clusters at the third level of the hierarchy. In this manner, American managers created the unifunctional structure, or departmental office, to manage the acquired or created reciprocally and sequentially interdependent elements. Following vertical integration, sequentially interdependent functions were grouped in a second level of the hierarchy to form the Stage II functional organization. After diversification, the heterogeneity of the environment forced a third-level grouping around pooled interdependent product, market, or geographic divisions.

Figure 2.3 Groupings by Interdependence Create a Hierarchy

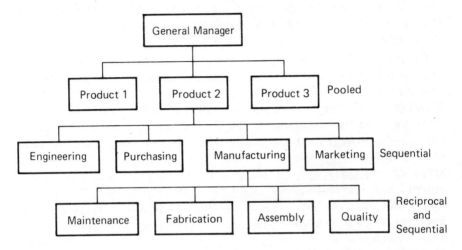

This structuring algorithm minimizes the coordination effort required to manage the interdependent elements.

Both Thompson and Williamson have generated conceptual contributions from which further theoretical and empirical work can continue. The compatibility of their concepts, Chandler's concepts, and the concepts used in business policy and organization design is striking. This is both encouraging and disheartening, however, because although a number of people are independently moving toward a consensus on strategy and structure, little of business policy thinking and language enters the other models, and vice versa.

The work of Thompson and Williamson illustrates the conceptual analysis stimulated by the publication of Chandler's book. They used Chandler as a source of data which both confirmed or modified their propositions and provided observations from which new propositions could be deduced. Another group of people used Chandler's work as a theoretical framework for their intuitive teachings as the basis for further empirical work. In the next chapter, we will review the empirical research that has accumulated over the last ten years following the publication of *Strategy and Structure*.

SUMMARY

This chapter has introduced the conceptual framework of strategy and structure. Specifically, the works of Chandler, Williamson, and Thompson are reviewed. All three present an interpretation of the relationship between strategy and structure.

Chandler suggests that as organizations change their growth strategy, new administrative problems arise that are solved when the organization structure is refashioned to fit the new strategy. This redesigning is necessary, because each structure facilitates a certain set of processes that also must fit the product-market strategy being pursued. The theoreticians suggest, then, that alternative organization forms make an economic difference.

The functional structure is seen as sufficient for providing the interunit coordination, specialization, and standardization needed to run an organization that has a single or dominant product-market strategy. This structure is created to handle the reciprocal and sequential interdependencies created by growth in volume and vertical integration, respectively. Therefore, the functional structure represents the first and second steps in the stagewise development of the firm.

The multi-divisional structure, an improved form for dealing with diversity, represents the third stage in an organization's growth. It is an attempt to deal with the third most crucial type of contingency: pooled interdependence. The decentralization of authority and responsibility allows for decision making at lower levels in the hierarchy. Almost all the resources needed to do a job are placed at the division's disposal. This structure permits quicker response to individual market demands by reducing need for communication and information processing. It also facilitates the capital allocation process by providing clear-cut appraisals and evaluations of both divisional performance and alternative investment proposals.

Viewed as a miniature capital market, the multi-divisional structure is superior to both the functional and holding company forms. The functional organization, which provides too few general managers, results in the inability to separate long-term strategic decisions from short-term operating decisions. The multi-divisional structure, however, creates a division of labor based on time, enabling divisions to concentrate on short-run operating decisions while the central office focuses upon strategic long-run decisions.

The holding company is viewed as being little different from the external capital market, because it is decentralized to the point that the central office makes decisions solely on the basis of financial performance. Hofer and Schendel elaborate further on these differences (Hofer and Schendel 1978).

This chapter, then, has presented three overall conceptual schemes that are intended to explain why organizations develop as they do. They provide a general framework with which to understand the chapters to follow. Specifically, the next chapter presents empirical studies that refine the concepts presented here and provide new data for further conceptualization.

3

Empirical Foundations of Strategy and Structure

This chapter reviews the research stimulated by Chandler. This work, which comes from the Industrial Development and Public Policy Program at the Harvard Business School and is summarized by Scott (1973), contributed several refinements and extensions of the Chandler thesis. First, it refined the theory of diversification strategy by distinguishing between different types of diversification (Wrigley 1970). Second, it demonstrated that not all multi-divisional structures are alike, by identifying different structural forms. Third, it quantified the analysis with data on financial performance (Rumelt 1973). The analysis was updated by extending the data base into 1970 for the U. S. (Rumelt 1973) and by carrying the analysis to European countries (Channon 1971; Pooley-Dyas 1972; Pavan 1972; Thanheiser 1972). Finally, it was extended to consider international strategies for American (Stopford and Wells 1973) and for European firms (Franco 1974 and 1977).

EMPIRICAL RESEARCH

The first study in this program of research refined the concept of diversification and compared the strategies with regard to structural form (Wrigley 1970). Taking a sample from the *Fortune 500*,

Wrigley distinguished four different strategies that were being followed. Some firms, such as the previously mentioned copper companies, stayed in a *single product business*. Another group diversified but still had a single *dominant business* that accounted for 70 to 95 percent of sales. An example of single dominant product business is the automobile industry. Still another group diversified but had more than 30 percent of their sales outside their main business in *related businesses*. The relation would be a common customer, a common distribution channel, or a common technology, for example. In any case, there was some connection among the products or businesses. Finally, the last group diversified into completely *unrelated businesses* and had more than 30 percent of their sales outside the main business. The structures that matched these strategies are shown in Table 3.1. From these data, it is clear that the more diversified the strategy, the more likely one is to find the multi-divisional structure. Single product or business firms are always organized functionally. Wrigley observed a hybrid form of structure also in use in the dominant business category. This group managed the dominant business through a functional structure and the diverse products through a divisionalized structure. This amounts to a partial move toward the multi-divisional structure. Those companies that diversified into related and unrelated businesses overwhelmingly chose multi-divisional structures. These results support the thesis that structure follows strategy in general, and that diversification leads to multi-divisional forms in particular.

Table 3.1 Strategy and Structure of Fortune 500 in 1967

Strategy	Percent Following Strategy	Functional Structure	Multi-divisional Structure
Single Business	6	6	0
Dominant Business	14	5	9
Related Business	60	3	57
Unrelated Business	20	0	20
TOTAL	100%	14%	86%

The same type of analysis was replicated for firms in the U. K. (Channon 1971), France (Pooley-Dyas 1972), Germany (Thanheiser 1972), and Italy (Pavan 1972, 1976). If structure follows strategy in the U. S., why not in Europe also? The results, which show some similarities and differences, are presented schematically in Figure 3.1. For all countries there is an increase in the amount of diversification between 1950 and 1970. Single and dominant business categories are substantial but declining. Similarly, there is an increase in the use of the multi-divisional structure at the expense of functional and holding company alternatives. However, there are variations across countries, and in all cases the diversification strategy is more extensive than the multi-divisional structure. The explanation offered is that diversification alone is not sufficient to bring about a reorganization of the power structure. It must be matched with competitive pressures. This is why the U. K. has gone further in implementing the multi-divisional structure than its continental neighbors. The decline of tariff barriers in the Common Market is now causing competition on the Continent. Along with competition comes the multi-divisional structure. Hence the current trend is observed and a prediction given that it will continue. Scott suggests that "the divisional structure appears to be the most effective way to manage the strategy of diversification under highly competitive conditions" (Scott 1973, p. 141). This view comes very close to Williamson's idea that the divisional structure performs competitive capital market functions effectively.

The last and most comprehensive example of this research is the study by Rumelt. He further elaborated the types of strategies of diversification. Through the use of subjective judgments and some quantitative measures, he created nine different strategies to characterize a sample of U. S. firms from the *Fortune 500*. The single business category remained as defined above, but the other three categories were elaborated.

The dominant product business (70 percent<dominant business sales<95 percent) was divided into four subcategories. The first subcategory was vertically integrated firms. These firms were classed as having sales outside the dominant business, but the products sold were by-products taken out of the sequential flow between stages of production. This strategy was different from those strategies involving independent businesses. The second, third, and fourth categories also apply as subclasses of the related business category. They characterize the degree of relatedness of the businesses into which the firm diversified. Some stayed "close to home" by adopt-

Figure 3.1 Evolution of Strategy and Structure in the Four Major Western European Countries, 1950–1970

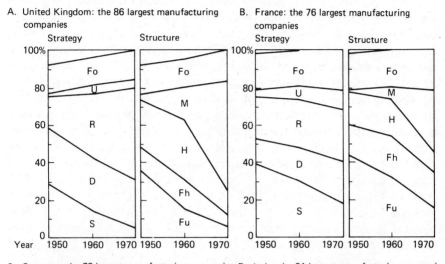

A. United Kingdom: the 86 largest manufacturing companies

B. France: the 76 largest manufacturing companies

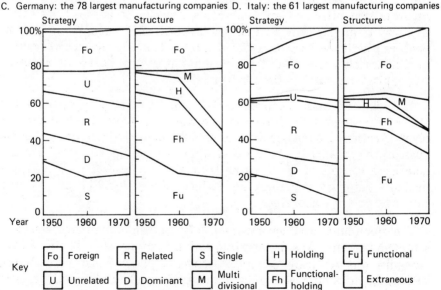

C. Germany: the 78 largest manufacturing companies   D. Italy: the 61 largest manufacturing companies

Key

| Fo | Foreign | R | Related | S | Single | H | Holding | Fu | Functional |
| U | Unrelated | D | Dominant | M | Multi divisional | Fh | Functional-holding | | Extraneous |

ing only products that utilized a common technology or market channel. These firms were classed as dominant-constrained. That is,
their diversification was constrained by the desire to exploit a particular advantage. The next type was a firm that diversified in a
manner that maintained links between businesses but was not constrained by one unifying link. That is, some products shared a common technology. Some of the technology sharers also shared a common distribution channel with another group of businesses. Viewed
as a whole, the businesses appear unrelated, but there are links of
varying types between all of them. This category was called
dominant-linked. The last category was simply dominant-unrelated;
it characterized firms diversifying into business totally unrelated
to the dominant and other businesses.

The related category, as suggested above, was divided into related-constrained and related-linked. The unrelated category was
also subdivided into two types. The purpose was to create a separate category for the acquisitive conglomerate. So the unrelateds
were classed on the basis of their aggressiveness in acquiring other
firms. This classification led to categories for the unrelated-passive
and the acquisitive conglomerate and made nine categories in all.

These strategies were then related to the type of structure. Rumelt
classed structures as being functional, functional with subsidiaries,
multi-divisional (both product and geographic divisions), and holding companies, the last being a divisional structure characterized by
highly autonomous divisions with a miniscule formal organization
above them. Strategies and structures employed by the sample were
examined from 1949 to 1969.

The results for strategies are shown in Figure 3.2 which demonstrates the decline of the single and dominant business categories
over the twenty-year period. The pattern of American business during that time was the strategy of product diversification. The results for the study of structure are shown in Figure 3.3.

As Chandler predicted, the multi-divisional form follows the diversification strategy. When strategy and structure are matched as in
Table 3.2, the Chandler thesis is again supported. The single and
dominant business strategies are conducted through functional organizations. The greater the diversity, the more likely one is to find
the multi-divisional form. Over time, an increasing percentage of
firms fall into step; by 1969, functional and holding company models
give way to the multi-divisional structure. Relations between strategy and structure eventually come into line, presumably because of
competitive pressures in the market.

Figure 3.2 Estimated Percentage of Firms in Each Strategic Class

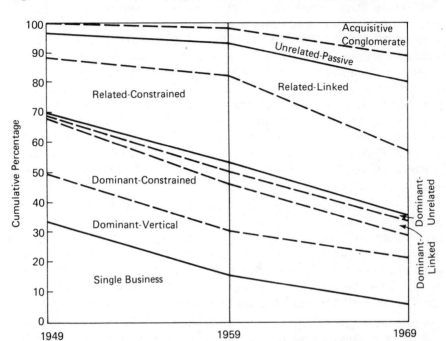

Rumelt also examined the financial performance of the firms in the sample in order to test strategy-structure-performance relations. First, economic performance and type of strategy were compared. The finding was that the type of diversification, not the amount, was related to economic performance. Both constrained strategies, dominant and related, were the top performers in almost all categories such as return on equity, stability, and various categories of growth. Thus, a strategy of controlled diversity is associated with high stable economic performance, because it neither commits the organization to a single business nor stretches it across industries. Instead, controlled diversity reflects the reason for the entry into related businesses: that all may draw upon a common strength or a distinctive competence. However, controlled diversity may not necessarily be the cause of economic performance; it may also result from it. The low performing related-constrained types may leave

Figure 3.3 Estimated Percentage of Firms in Each Organizational Class, 1949–1969

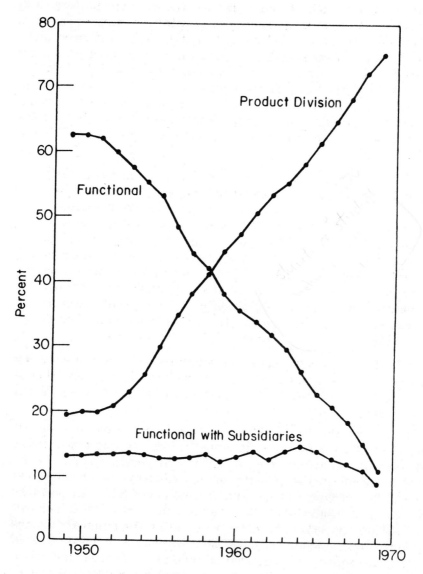

to try related-linked businesses, leaving the high performing related-constrained firms. Cause and effect statements cannot be made yet.

The multi-divisional structure per se was the high performer in all growth areas and in risk-adjusted growth in earnings per share. It had average return on equity and capital. This finding is interesting, because often growth is assumed to be purchased at the expense of reduced profitability. Instead, growth and profitability were positively related, and the multi-divisional firms were able to increase profits faster than functional organizations while maintaining the same return on capital. The reason is assumed to be the planning, control, and reward systems used in multi-divisional structures.

> Unlike many functionally organized firms, and particularly unlike a vertically integrated firm, the diversified divisionalized company does not have to reinvest in marginal activities just to "stay in the game"; its strategy permits, and its structure facilitates, a range of policies tailored to individual businesses. Some areas can be used as cash generators or dropped entirely; others may provide stable long term performance and still others may consist of risky, but potentially lucrative new ventures. As a result, there is less conflict on the corporate level between the goals of profitability and growth. (Rumelt 1973, p. 126).

Again, it is not only the divisional structure but also the matching of processes and systems to strategy, as well as to the achievement of short-run profit in the divisions and long-term growth overall, that is important.

The tests of the fit of strategy-structure-performance were not conclusive. Two tests were attempted. First, it was hypothesized that in science-based industries divisionalized structures would be superior to nondivisionalized structures. Actually, the reverse was found to be true but was not regarded as significant. In part, the test was invalid because of the rare occurrence of nondivisionalized firms. There appear to be other reasons for the minimal findings in this part of Rumelt's study. First, science-based firms do well, in general, independent of organization structure. Second, there is a comparison of firms at different stages of development in the product life cycle. Thus, firms such as Kodak or Abbott Laboratories had well-developed major product lines; as long as firms have a winner, they get growth and high returns. Rumelt found no examples of science-based firms with products in the mature or the declining phases of the product life cycle that had not diversified and adopted multi-

Table 3.2 Strategy and Structure Among the Top 500

	Percentage in Each Structural Class				
Strategic Class	Functional	Functional with Subsidiaries	Product Division	Geographic Division	Holding Company
1949					
Single	90.7	4.0	2.7	1.3	1.3
Dominant	56.8	23.2	17.1	0	2.9
DV	61.9	25.3	12.9	0	0
DC	53.1	18.8	22.4	0	5.6
DL + DU	50.0	50.0	0	0	0
Related	42.2	14.2	40.3	0	3.3
RC	49.0	17.8	30.9	0	2.3
RL	26.2	5.5	62.7	0	5.5
Unrelated	0	0	61.2	0	38.8
UP	0	0	61.2	0	38.8
AC	–	–	–	–	–
1959					
Single	90.6	5.8	0	3.6	0
Dominant	36.4	22.4	34.5	4.2	2.5
DV	41.7	20.8	34.5	3.0	0
DC	46.1	20.9	25.6	4.3	3.1
DL + DU	0	29.5	96.9	6.8	6.8
Related	20.1	8.3	79.6	0	0
RC	26.1	9.9	64.0	0	0
RL	4.0	4.0	92.0	0	0
Unrelated	0	0	93.3	0	6.7
UP	0	0	91.8	0	8.2
AC	0	0	100.0	0	0
1969					
Single	62.3	14.2	14.2	9.3	0
Dominant	20.7	17.5	60.3	1.5	0
DV	32.2	22.6	45.2	0	0
DC	14.2	6.2	73.5	6.2	0
DL + DU	0	17.8	82.2	0	0
Related	2.9	6.6	89.5	1.0	0
RC	4.1	9.7	86.3	0	0
RL	1.9	3.7	92.5	1.9	0
Unrelated	0	2.3	85.3	0	12.4
UP	0	5.2	94.8	0	0
AC	0	0	77.8	0	22.2

divisional structures. A third interpretation draws on the competition variable introduced by Scott. In the early phases of their life, new high-technology products enjoy monopoly status. They will produce profit independent of organizational structure. This view suggests that performance causes diversification (strategy) and structure; the change is provoked by decline in performance. Finally, if a firm is not exceptionally large, it can institutionalize innovation in a functional organization with limited product diversity and draw upon its specialists, who thrive on the functional form. Rumelt's research, however, did not control for some type of product overlay such as business teams or product managers in a functionally dominant form, even though the latter forms are common in moderately sized functional organizations (Corey and Star 1971; Galbraith 1973).

Rumelt's second test controlled for strategy. Within the related strategies (constrained and linked), it was hypothesized that the multi-divisional would outperform the functional organization. Partial support for this proposition was found. Return on equity, return on capital, and price earnings ratios were higher, but they were not statistically significant. Growth in earnings per share, which was higher for functional organizations, was also not statistically significant. The only significant difference was that multidivisionals produced higher sales growth. So, four out of five hypotheses were in the predicted direction, and one was significant. This is supportive but not overwhelming evidence.

In summary, the Rumelt study caps the Harvard research that shows the diversification of large firms in the Western world and the continuing adoption of the multi-divisional form to manage that diversity. The program supports the thesis that structure follows strategy but fortunately raises as many questions as it answers. The failure to show that high performance comes from a match of strategy and structure suggests that either controls on life cycles are needed, or that economic performance is independent of strategy-structure congruence. Large samples, longitudinal data, and sophisticated, time phased econometric techniques are needed.

THE INTERNATIONAL STUDIES

A second program of research, the Harvard International Project, has also generated a good deal of empirical study relevant to strategy and structure linkages (Fouraker and Stopford 1968; Stopford 1968; Stopford and Wells 1973; Franko 1974, 1977). This group has followed the changes in structure that have accompanied strategies of international expansion for U. S. and European firms.

Stopford studied a sample of U. S. firms taken again from the *Fortune 500*. To qualify, a firm had to have six manufacturing subsidiaries in foreign countries in 1963 in which it had at least 25 percent ownership. These were firms that expanded internationally during the 1950s, largely exploiting technological innovations to overcome lower labor costs elsewhere. These firms were classified using the Stage I, II (functional), and III (multi-divisional) categories. The type of structure and degree of domestic product diversification, measured as percentage of sales outside the primary industry, are shown in Table 3.3. The data show the previously discussed effects of diversity. There are no functional organizations with more than 6 percent of their revenues coming from outside their primary industry. In addition, it shows that the divisionalized companies were the ones that adopted an international strategy. The multi-divisionals also had the greatest expenditures of research and development and could exploit the technical advantage.

Table 3.3 Structure and the Degree of Domestic Product Diversification

Total Product Diversification (%)	Structure	
	Stage II	Stage III
0	12	19
1–6	5	14
7–17	–	17
18–45	–	37
46–71	–	35
	17	122

SOURCE: Stopford 1968, p. 45.

Stopford traces these firms as they expanded internationally during the 1960s. In so doing, he finds that American firms adopted common structures when following common strategies. The first major structural change adopted by the firms was the establishment of an international division that was added to the existing product divisionalized structure. This form is shown in Figure 3.4.

This form was adopted universally for several reasons. First, it brought together all international activities that were individually insignificant and often neglected in favor of higher priority domestic concerns when they were scattered throughout the divisions. Collectively, these pieces could constitute a $10 to $20 million business and

Figure 3.4 Product Divisionalized Firm with an International Division

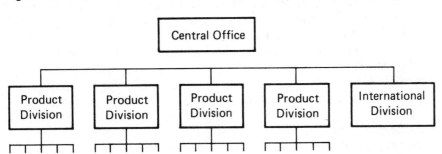

receive their just deserts. Second, the international division was a span-of-control reducer for the chief executive of firms that grew by acquisition and had three or more foreign subsidiaries reporting to the top. And finally, it economized on a scarce resource—internationally experienced general managers. Thus, the initial structural response was to create an international division that differentiated all international activity from domestic business.

The international division was a transitory form, however, and gave way to another, more global form. Which global form a company moved to depended on the firm's international growth strategy. Those firms that took their entire diversified domestic product line abroad would eventually adopt worldwide product divisions. Those firms that expanded internationally with only their dominant business adopted geographic divisions that divided the world into areas. Each of these strategies set up forces that led to the abandonment of the international division. Let us look at these strategies and see why each led to new structures.

Diversification in foreign markets eventually led to the worldwide product division. This conclusion is developed from data contained in Tables 3.4 and 3.5. They show that Stage II firms have low diversity abroad as well as at home. Next, Stage III firms with an international division are concentrated among those with low foreign product diversity (i. e., percent sales outside the primary industry in foreign markets). Only eight out of forty-eight have more than 5 percent of their sales outside their main business. Organization forms classed as Other are either product divisions, area divisions, or mixed forms. Other forms that were adopted are shown in Table 3.5.

The worldwide product divisionalized firms have high diversity, the area division firms do not. The mixed forms are scattered throughout. The question now becomes, Why is the international division

Table 3.4 Foreign Product Diversity and Stage of Development

Foreign Product Diversity %	Stage II	Stage III with Int. Division	Stage III Other
0	13	26	7
1–5	4	14	7
6–25	–	5	10
26–71	–	3	12
Total	17	48	36

SOURCE: Stopford 1968, p. 47

Table 3.5 Foreign Product Diversity and Organizational Form

Foreign Product Diversification %	World Wide Product Div.	Area Division	Mixed Form
0	1	5	1
1–5	1	2	4
6–25	7	1	2
26–71	8	1	2
Total	17	9	9

SOURCE: Stopford 1968, p. 64

abandoned at high levels of diversity, and a worldwide product division adopted?

Stopford's explanation is the Chandler thesis that one cannot manage diversity within a single structure, be it functional or, in this case, geographic. That is, the international division was usually organized geographically, and the European and Latin American departments had to manage the entire diversified product line. A typical structure is shown in Figure 3.5. The countries reported to regions which in turn reported to the international headquarters. These organizations then gradually increased the amount of product diversity in foreign markets. As new products were added, the additional administrative load burdened the executives in regional and international offices. Usually, they reverted to what they knew best—managing the first product line introduced in international markets. The newly introduced products experienced difficulty and thereby triggered a reorganization. Some firms used an intermediate step of international product departments shown in Figure 3.6.

Then, when the vice-president of the international division moved on, the departments were distributed among the respective domestic product divisions, which assumed worldwide responsibility. Thus,

Figure 3.5 Structure of the International Division

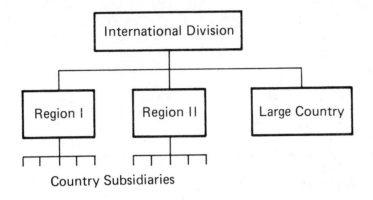

Country Subsidiaries

Figure 3.6 International Division Organized by Product

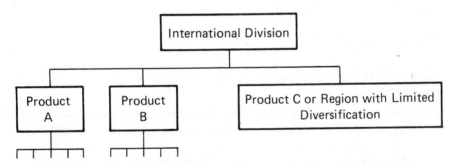

structure follows strategy. Product diversity is best managed through product divisionalized firms.

The next question is, Why did the international division disappear for firms that did not diversify abroad but grew in a dominant business? One reason might be that geographic diversity presents the same problems as product diversity and overloads the executive, who is trying to manage multiple countries and regions. However, Stopford's data do not show that geographic diversity leads to the abandonment of the international division and the adoption of the area divisions. In part, this result is expected because the international division itself was already organized on a geographic basis, as shown in Figure 3.5. Thus, it was already prepared to manage this source of diversity.

The explanation offered by Stopford is a political one based on two observations. First, area divisionalized firms had the highest percentage of total revenue coming from foreign sources. (It is important that it is percentage of total sales and not the absolute amount). These data are shown in Table 3.6. The area divisionalized firms have an average of 45.6 percent of sales coming from overseas.

Table 3.6 Organization Structure and Foreign Sales

Structure	Percentage of Total Sales from Foreign Sales
Area Division	45.6
Mixed	30.7
Stage II	26.7
Stage III with international division	20.8
Worldwide product division	17.4
All firms	25.4

(Adapted from Stopford 1968, p. 101).

A second and more detailed observation was that the area division was adopted at a time when the international division grew to a size equal to the largest U. S. domestic division. It was therefore hypothesized that a coalition of the domestic divisions caused the breakup of the international division, which was beginning to get the lion's share of the capital and research and development budget, and the managerial talent and other resources. The explanation is post hoc and has not been directly tested. However, it fits with numerous case study interpretations.

The results of Stopford's work are shown graphically in Figure 3.7. The Stage II firms and the Stage III firms with an international division are all located inside the boundary running between 10 percent diversification and 50 percent foreign sales. With an increase in sales or diversification or both, the firm crosses the boundary, abandons the international division, and adopts a global Stage III form. Which form is adopted depends on the growth strategy pursued by the firm. Sales growth in a dominant product line leads to area divisions. Diversification in foreign as well as domestic markets leads to worldwide product divisions. Again, structure follows strategy, this time in the international context.

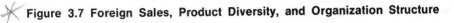

Figure 3.7 Foreign Sales, Product Diversity, and Organization Structure

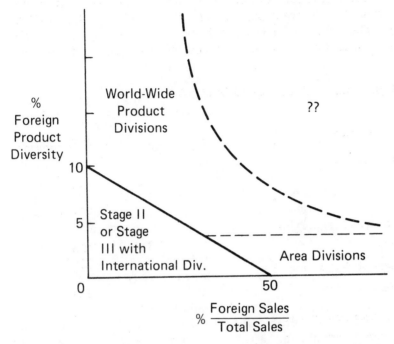

Stopford raises an interesting question that is not answered by his data. What happens as area divisionalized firms diversify, or world-wide product firms increase foreign sales? Some mixed forms were observed where the firm had area divisions, but one large and unique product had been organized as a worldwide product division. One of Stopford's firms had been organized as a matrix or grid form by simultaneously assuming a geographic and a product form. This type will be treated later in more detail. For the moment the question of What lies on the other side of the next boundary? is the state-of-the-art question. We will return to it later.

The above data apply to American firms in the 1950s and 1960s. One is led to question the experience of other multi-nationals during the same period. Franko has done exactly that by examining the experience of European firms taken from the *Fortune 200* for European companies during the same period (Franko 1974, 1977). His initial findings did not support the Chandler thesis. The vast majority of European multi-nationals in 1961 were organized around an international holding company/domestic functional model, which Franko labeled the mother-daughter form. This form was used even when

Figure 3.8 The International Holding Company/Domestic Functional Form (Mother-Daughter)

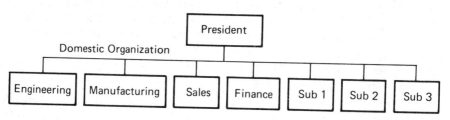

the multi-nationals pursued product diversification. The mother organization located in the country of ownership was organized functionally. The top functional managers, as well as all the subsidiary presidents, reported directly to the president as shown in Figure 3.8. In one case, the president had the presidents of all seventy-five subsidiary companies reporting to him directly. The question arises, How can they control considerable product and geographic diversity using the mother-daughter form, if American firms have to use a Stage III multi-divisional form? And how do they manage product diversity in domestic markets using a functional organization? Franko suggests that these firms discovered ways to eliminate the need for cross-border strategies and cross-border and cross-product information transmission by establishing a personal control structure (as opposed to the impersonal performance oriented U. S. structures), by marketing known products, and by eliminating competition. Let us look at each of these and consider their combined effect.

The personal control structure of the mother-daughter form was based on the use of home country expatriates as a substitute for the rules, procedures, job descriptions, performance reporting, and standard formats used by American companies. Instead, the organization sent a trusted member of the community who had proved himself at home. The expatriate had years of acculturation at headquarters, came from the ruling families, and had a class background similar to that of the top management. Then so long as social constraints were respected and dividend expectations met, there was little need to transfer information; little need for contact between headquarters and the subsidiaries; and hence, little need for narrow spans of control. These firms substituted socialization of managers for the use of impersonal control mechanisms (Edström and Galbraith 1977).

The nature of the markets facilitated this loosely coupled structure. These firms marketed known products with high price elasticities. Therefore, the key information to support decisions was local price data. Decision makers needed primarily local knowledge of markets and prices. In addition, competition in these markets was successfully eliminated. Tariff barriers and close ties to governments separated markets and eliminated outsiders. Then, the "competitors" formed agreements and cartels to eliminate the remainder of the competitive threat. These informal arrangements were facilitated by the common social class backgrounds of competitors and by the lack of antitrust laws or the enforcement of existing laws. Collectively, these arrangements permitted the mother-daughter form to exist by eliminating the need for cross-border and cross-product information transmission. These organizations were held together not by an international strategy but by common social class and common upbringing.

The introduction to this section was prefaced by saying that Franko's results *initially* failed to support the Chandler thesis. The reason is that the mother-daughter form is disappearing. By 1971, the numbers of mother-daughter forms had dropped from sixty-one out of seventy in 1961 to twenty-five out of seventy. More revealing is the observation that between 1968 and 1972, forty-four firms changed their structures to the multi-divisional structure. Why? Franko suggests that it is the breakdown of the negotiated environment. The breakdown is the combination of several factors. First, beginning in 1968, the tariff barriers in the Common Market dropped to zero, thereby exposing national companies to outside competition. Many of these national companies merged to fight the intrusion of outsiders in their local domains. Second, new groups of outsiders such as Americans and Japanese joined other European firms in the entrance into the local market. These outsiders did not know the rules of gentlemanly conduct and often cut price to gain market share. And finally, some countries and the EEC began to legislate and enforce antitrust action. This antitrust action eliminated the cartel response to competition. Thus, antitrust action, new competitors, and declining tariff barriers began to destroy the negotiated environment.

The strength of Franko's case rests on the fact that the environment did not change equally in all countries or in all industries. The largest number of and earliest changes to multi-divisional forms occurred in the U. K., the country with the least government planning, the most antitrust enforcement, and the greatest penetration by non-European companies. French companies show the least percentage of companies changing to multi-divisional forms. France has the most central planning and least penetration by outside firms. Similarly, in the pharmaceutical and chemical industries, where the largest number of antitrust suits exists and where the only two fines have occurred, all fourteen companies have adopted the multi-divisional structure. The greater the penetration by outside competitors and the greater the amount of antitrust activity, the more likely one is to find a move toward the multi-divisional structure. In industries where the same negotiated environment exists, the functional and holding company models are still used.

Thus, country and industry comparisons add further support to the case that diversity combined with competition leads to the multi-divisional form. Neither alone is sufficient to provoke a change to the new structure. The European data analyzed by the Harvard group and by Franko extend the Chandler thesis to account for the competitive environment in which the strategy and structure linkage takes place. It appears that structure follows strategy only when structure makes a difference. When diversifying under monopoly conditions, however, strategy can be implemented independent of structure. The status quo structure offers the solution with the least resistance. It is only when competition causes performance deterioration that structural adjustment is needed to restore profits to acceptable levels.

In summary, the international studies extend the range of observations over some new strategies and into new national contexts. In general, the results support the argument that structure follows strategy. Firms pursuing different strategies adopt predictably different structures. The data for European firms build on Scott's earlier suggestion about the importance of competition. Both diversification and competitive markets are needed to provoke a major structural change. Collectively, the studies leave us hypothesizing about the relations between strategy, structure, economic performance, and competitiveness of markets.

STRATEGY, STRUCTURE
AND FINANCIAL PERFORMANCE

The empirical evidence presented above certainly supports the hypothesis that strategy and structure are related. With due regard for competition, diversification leads to the multi-divisional structure. However, it has not yet been demonstrated that structure contributes to economic performance or that firms that have matched strategy and structure perform better than those that have not. In this section, we will review the few studies that have explicitly related structure or strategy and structure to financial performance.

Throughout the above discussion, the implicit assumption was that in order to be economically effective, strategy and structure must be matched. The fact that under competitive conditions very few mismatches occur is taken as evidence supporting the assumption. Although the nonexistence of mismatches supports this premise, it does not eliminate alternative explanations. One can also point to some, albeit few, mismatches that do exist. Also, there is no indication of the importance of the match to financial success. If there is a relation but its magnitude is small, then managers should concentrate elsewhere for improving performance. A few studies have addressed these questions.

The Rumelt study discussed above was the first to examine the economic consequences explicitly. Rumelt recognized that success could result from pursuing good strategies, from adopting a good structure, or from creating a match between the two. Recall that he found that strategies resulted in varying degrees of success, with the related businesses performing best. The multi-divisional structure was the best performer for growth and had average returns on equity and capital. Growth and returns were also positively related, showing that the multi-divisional structure could achieve growth without sacrificing profitability. The fit test was performed only on organizations that had diversified. Here, on four out of five financial measures, the mismatches (functional) performed below those firms that had matched the diversification strategy with a multi-divisional structure. Only on one measure was the difference statistically significant. However, there was no attempt at an analysis of variance to determine the relative contribution of strategy, structure, or fit.

Parts of the Rumelt research have been replicated by Channon in a study of British service industry firms such as banks, insurance companies, and hotels (1977). Using the categories of single business, dominant business, diversification into related businesses, and diversification into unrelated businesses, he found that the single and related business categories were superior on a number of measures of growth and returns, with the related businesses being marginally superior overall. This suggests that diversification is pursued only after the single business begins to decline. If prospects are good, no diversification occurs. When diversification does occur, however, greater success is achieved by going into related businesses, as opposed to unrelated ones.

The structure results were somewhat similar to Rumelt's. The multi-divisional firms had high growth results for sales, assets, and earnings per share while maintaining above average returns. The functional organizations had slightly higher returns, and holding companies were the poorest performers. Unfortunately, there was no test for the fit between strategy and structure.

Another study tested the effects of using a profit center structure, presumably a multi-divisional, versus not using one, presumably a functional organization (Poensgen 1974). Using financial data taken from Compustat tapes and structure categories from a questionnaire (Mauriel and Anthony 1966), correlations with controls for factors such as size and industry were computed for 364 American firms. The result shows that profit center structures are more profitable, with structure explaining about 10 percent of the variance in return on equity. This is one of the few measures of importance and indicates that structure can have an effect of up to 10 percent. Cause and effect analyses yielded no results. Before and after data did not show an increase in profitability after going to the profit center structure. Finally, Rumelt's results of low association between returns and growth for profit centers were reproduced. Presumably with one group working on returns (divisions) and one group working on growth (corporate), the association between the two is less. Growth, in a multi-divisional structure, does not depend on profit from current operations to the degree that it does in a functional organization.

The last study to be reported here examined the economic performance of eighty-two British firms (Cable and Speer 1977). The primary independent variable was optimal organization form. Optimal forms are multi-divisional forms, with separation of division and corporate interests based on time horizon, and functional organizations in a single business. Nonoptimal are holding companies, multi-divisionals with corporate offices too involved in division activities, and diversified functional forms. Controlling for size, industry, ownership, and growth, the authors found that organization form is a significant predictor of return on equity and assets. Organization can account for between 7 percent and 9 percent difference in returns. Overall, the authors explain about 50 percent of the variance. Unfortunately, the criteria for determining the optimal organization are not explicit. However, the inclusion of several regressions with questionable cases omitted or reclassified produces little change in overall results. Some care should be taken in interpreting the authors' conclusion that organization makes a difference. Involvement by corporate superiors may be a response to, not a cause of, poor performance. The nonoptimal classification distorts the effect of organization. The results, like those of other correlation studies, should be interpreted with respect to causation.

In summary, there is some correlation evidence that structure and economic performance are related. However, causal interpretations cannot be made from the correlation data. Also, there is no strong proof that a fit between strategy and structure leads to effective performance. The data do not permit rejection of the fit hypothesis either, however. Much of the data supports it, but there are still alternative explanations that cannot be rejected.

SUMMARY

This chapter has outlined the empirical studies that have been stimulated by Chandler's work. Various types of diversification strategies and organizational structures are identified. Hypotheses concerning the strategy-structure relationship, the strategy-structure-competition relationship, and the relationships of the above variables versus economic performance variables are tested. The tests are conducted on American, European, and international organizations.

General support is found for Chandler's major thesis that organization structure follows its growth strategy. However, several refinements have been made. One such refinement concerns the explication of competition as an important variable. Studies conducted in Europe indicated that diversification strategies outnumbered multi-divisional structures. Apparently, diversification must also be matched by competitive pressures in order for the thesis to hold. Another refinement involves the inclusion of financial data into the empirical tests.

Rumelt recently conducted a comprehensive study that categorized nine different types of diversification strategies. The study also classified structures as functional, functional with subsidiaries, multi-divisional, and holding company. The results show the decline of the single and dominant product-market strategies over a twenty-year period. It also illustrated how the functional and holding company forms had given way to the multi-divisional structure.

Rumelt's performance data indicated that controlled diversity, which reflects businesses that all draw upon a common strength or distinctive competence, is the one associated with high stable economic performance. Similarly, the multi-divisional structure is the high performer in almost all financial areas. The reason is assumed to be the planning, control, and reward system used in the multi-divisional structure. The structure facilitates a range of policies tailored to individual businesses. So again, it is not just the divisional structure that is important, but also the matching of processes and systems to strategy. Rumelt failed, however, to show conclusively that the fit between strategy and structure was an important predictor of financial performance. The lack of findings in this area could have been caused by methodological problems concerning the nature of the sample and by the sample size. Other plausible explanations include a failure to look at the internal processes and at alternative mechanisms for coordination.

Finally, a third major refinement of Chandler's thesis has been provided by studies done on international organizations. These studies, which provide further elaborations of Chandler's concept of stages of growth, emphasize again the importance of a competitive environment.

Having presented some major refinements of Chandler's thesis and of the conceptualization presented in chapter 1, we move to the next chapter, which helps to clarify what has been introduced thus far. Chapter 4 does so by including an actual case and by reviewing other studies that look at the strategy-structure relationship from a slightly different perspective.

4

Strategy, Structure, and Organizational Processes

In this chapter we will discuss a number of other studies that have contributed to our understanding of relationships between strategy and structure. Many were not directly motivated by Chandler's work but are relevant to the questions raised by his work. Since the studies were performed for other reasons, some translation into the strategy-structure perspective is needed. These studies contribute to our understanding, because they introduce some different structural dimensions such as decentralization and relate them to strategy. In addition to structure, they greatly elaborate the organizational variables into areas of reward and evaluation, cross-departmental teams, and planning and information systems. These additions allow us to study organizations as the rich, complex entities that they are.

GALBRAITH'S BOEING STUDY

The study of the Commercial Airplane Division (CAD) of the Boeing Company by Galbraith provides a transition into this new area (Galbraith 1971). By means of a retrospective case study, Galbraith traced the changes in the airplane market, Boeing's strategy, and the structure of the CAD from the mid-1950s to 1967. In general, the market became more competitive, the CAD first diversified by adding new airplane programs and then changed from a functional to a divisionalized structure.

Boeing entered the commercial aircraft market with the 707, a derivative of the KC–135 military plane. Their strategy was to "make a market" for jet aircraft where only propeller aircraft had existed before. They built a prototype 707 and took orders from airlines after they observed it. The 707 was successful, and other companies introduced their own models (DC–8 and Convair 880) to compete directly on intercontinental flights. Next, Boeing introduced the 727 to "make a market" on intermediate-length flights (e. g., Chicago to New York). Again the approach was slow and deliberate. Instead of building a prototype, they spent years in the wind tunnel to perfect the three aftmounted engine configuration. Again the effort was successful. These programs were managed through the division's functional organization.

The market changed significantly in the mid-1960s. Douglas did not introduce a competing product to the 727. Instead, they introduced the DC–9, a short-haul aircraft (e. g., New York to Washington). The entire market exploded at that time, as more airlines entered more submarkets. The strategy was no longer to "make a market"; the market existed, and the problem was to get to it quickly. Boeing introduced various 727 models, the short-haul 737, the SST, and the 747 after they lost the C–5A military contract. Boeing no longer had the luxury of time and no longer had a temporary monopoly position. The new models spent only several months in the wind tunnel. The effects of shortened schedules and competition began to show. The 737 program began to fall behind schedule. Other financial problems developed, because the Vietnam build-up diverted resources to defense needs. At this time, Douglas failed and was purchased by McDonnell Corporation.

Boeing survived the squeeze. They reorganized the CAD into a divisionalized structure. One division was created for each model, the 707 and 727, the 737, the 747, and the SST. A central fabricating division that supplied to other divisions was also created. This structure remained for several years and helped Boeing adapt to the new market, the diverse programs, and the increased competition.

The study suffers, as all case studies do, from confounded changes. There were changes in the market, the number of programs, the financial transactions (the government made progress payments and the airlines did not), and the size of the organization. However, the developments at Boeing can be interpreted in the structure-follows-strategy framework. Boeing adopted a strategy of introducing new products into existing competitive markets and adopted a divisionalized structure to implement it. The structure was adopted only after a decrease in performance provoked the move. Previously, the "make a market" strategy gave them a temporary monopoly position that was managed through a functional organization. The market change and the increase in the number of airplane programs and customers all combined to render the functional organization obsolete. At a minimum, the case cannot reject the Chandler thesis and even lends support to it when combined with the other studies.

DIVERSITY AND DECENTRALIZATION

Many of the studies to be cited in this and later sections focus on the structural dimension of decentralization. This dimension was implicit in many of the aforementioned studies. Chandler spoke of the centralized functional organization and the decentralized multi-divisional form. However, within any multi-divisional form there is the choice of the amount of divisional autonomy that is appropriate for the implementation of strategy. Two studies have directly addressed the question of autonomy and strategy.

Berg addressed the question of structural differences in explaining why the conglomerates of the 1960s were effective (1965). He noted that there were two types of divisional structures, the conglomerate and the diversified majors. The diversified majors, which were the multi-divisional type of form described by Chandler, usually had several hundred people in the corporate office. They coordinated divisional activity through corporate policies and direct participation of corporate offices. In contrast, the conglomerate, similar to the holding company, would have ten to twenty general managers with specialists only in the tax, legal, and financial areas. The conglomerate, then, placed nearly all functions within the division and eliminated the need for coordination. Corporate divisional interests were coordinated through the reward system.

The greater decentralization in the conglomerate case was justified, because they managed greater diversity. Berg describes them as diversifying into unrelated businesses, to use Rumelt's categories. The diversified majors were less diverse and followed a strategy of diversifying into related businesses. The relatedness of these divisions required some coordination in the corporate interest, thereby necessitating more corporate management. Thus, greater diversity of a quantitative and qualitative nature requires greater divisional autonomy and smaller corporate offices.

The second study that addresses the issue is based on an empirical study of six divisionalized firms (Lorsch and Allen 1973). The firms varied in the degree of diversity, the degree of uncertainty, and the amount of interdivisional trading. Indeed, two firms had sufficient interdivisional transfers to be called vertically integrated. The other four firms were classed as conglomerates. Lorsch and Allen measured a number of dimensions of organization, some of which will be dealt with more fully below. The concern here is with the size of the corporate offices, the functions performed at corporate offices, and the degree of divisional autonomy. Table 4.1 shows data relevant to the first two questions.

Three of the conglomerates fit the pattern suggested by Berg. They had small corporate offices and performed few divisional functions. The one conglomerate that operated as a vertically integrated firm was also the poorest performer. The vertically integrated units, in contrast, were larger, performed more corporate functions, and served in some operating as well as policy roles in these functions.

Lorsch and Allen also measured the amount of integrating effort expended at corporate offices on corporate-divisional relations and interdivisional relations. The lower performing vertically integrated firm was shown to spend too little effort in integrating the interdependent divisions. On the other hand, the lower performing conglomerates were characterized by too much integrative effort. Some effort is surely attributable to lower performance per se, but the conclusion is that strategies characterized by diversity and uncertainty require greater decentralization and self-containment of divisions. When autonomy is not given, lower performance results. Strategies leading to interdivisional interdependence, such as vertical integration, require more corporate integrative effort. When too little is given, lower performance results. The extent of decentralization follows from the strategy.

CONTINGENCY THEORIES
OF ORGANIZATIONS

The field of organization theory should have a great deal to contribute to questions of strategy and structure linkages. However, the amount of relevant work falls short of one's expectations. Only recently have

Table 4.1 Basic Characteristics of Corporate Headquarters Units in Six Firms [a]

	Conglomerate Firms			Vertically Integrated Firms		
	1	2	3	4	5	6
A. Size—total number of management and professional employees	17	20	25	230	479	250
B. Functions performed in Reference to divisions						
1. Financial/control	X_p	X_p	X_p	X_p	$X_{o,p}$	$X_{o,p}$
2. Long-range planning	X_p	X_p	X_p	X_p	$X_{o,p}$	$X_{o,p}$
3. Legal	$X_{o,p}$	$X_{o,p}$	$X_{o,p}$	$X_{o,p}$	$X_{o,p}$	$X_{o,p}$
4. Industrial relations	$X_{o,p}$	$X_{o,p}$	$X_{o,p}$	$X_{o,p}$	$X_{o,p}$	$X_{o,p}$
5. Operations research					X_p	
6. Marketing		X_p	X_p	X_o	X_o	X_o
7. Manufacturing/industrial engineering			X_p	X_p		
8. Planning and scheduling of output					X_o	X_o
9. Purchasing					X_o	X_o
10. Engineering (other than industrial)				X_p		
11. Research and development				$X_{o,p}$	X_o	X_o

[a] X indicates that certain functions in specified areas are performed by the headquarters unit for the divisions. P indicates that corporate involvement is of a policy setting nature; i. e., setting policies, advising, providing basic approaches. O indicates an operating responsibility for the headquarters unit; e. g., actually carrying out some purchasing activities for certain divisions.

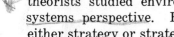

theorists studied environmental linkages through a so-called open systems perspective. Even then they have not directly addressed either strategy or strategy-structure relations. However, some of the work is relevant and is briefly reviewed here.

The portion of organization theory that is relevant to considerations of strategy and structure is the work usually summarized as contingency theory. The theory states that there is no one best way of organizing, but that all ways of organizing are not equally effective. That is, the choice of organization form makes a difference in terms of economic performance. The choice depends, however, on the situation. Therefore, contingency theorists have concentrated on situational attributes that make a difference.

The initial impetus came from British sociologists. Joan Woodward proposed that manufacturing technology was a primary determinant of organization form (1965). Subsequent research has substantiated some of her original findings and modified others (Hinings et al. 1969; Child and Mansfield 1972; Blau et al. 1975). In general, the impact of production technology per se is limited to the manufacturing function; and, the lower the level in the structure, the stronger the impact. As a result, this school of thought is not of primary concern.

Two other British sociologists suggested that it was the rate of change of the environment that determined organization form (Burns and Stalker 1961). They suggested that in industries characterized by high rates of change of markets and technology, successful firms adopted what they called an "organic form." An organic organization was decentralized with ambiguous roles and a great deal of lateral communication. In industries with stable markets and product lines, the firms adopted a mechanistic organization. This form was characterized by centralization and well-defined roles, with communication following the chain of command. This form was hypothesized to be successful for the stable markets. Thus, the type of organization (structure) is contingent upon the rate of change in the environment (strategy). Those firms in high technology industries and in markets characterized by rapid change following strategies of new product introduction, such as the semiconductor industry, should adopt decentralized organic forms.

The results of these studies, when combined with emerging contingency theories of leadership (Fiedler 1967), small group processes (Leavitt 1962), preindustrial societies (Udy 1959), and Chandler, gave impetus to the belief that a new discovery was in the making. A great deal of research then followed from these original studies. Some work was conceptual (Perrow 1967; Thompson 1967); some research was empirical (Hall 1961; Hage and Aiken 1969); and other studies concentrated upon measuring uncertainty (Duncan 1971; Van de Ven and Delbecq 1975). The rationale for contingency theory, however, was established by the publication of *Organization and Environment* by Lawrence and Lorsch in 1969.

The Lawrence and Lorsch study examined ten firms in three different industries. There are several portions to their research, but one piece is directly relevant here. They showed that high performing firms in an uncertain environment had greater decentralization than low performers, and that in the predictable industry, the high performer was the more centralized. The high performers in both industries had achieved a fit with their environment. The addition of the performance measures gave contingency theory the necessary credibility. Textbooks have now picked up the results of the study, and contingency theory is the dominant school of thought in organization behavior.

Subsequent to the publication of the work of Lawrence and Lorsch, several other studies have followed and measured performance. These will be discussed in a later section of this chapter. In summary, organization theorists have adopted their own contingency theory of structure. Instead of focussing upon strategy, they have considered various dimensions of the task to be performed. Usually, task uncertainty is the dimension that is to vary with organization structure. This point of view is consistent with the Chandler hypothesis, since uncertainty and diversity tend to vary together. These studies give still more weight to the strategy-structure thesis.

COMPETITIVENESS AND STRUCTURE

Organization theorists have done some work on the competitiveness issue. Recall that Scott, Rumelt, and Franko all relied on competitiveness to explain why the multi-divisional structure was not adopted by all firms pursuing strategies of product diversification. There are no studies that directly examine this relation, but there are several that have examined the degree of competition in an industry and its effect on structure.

Some discussion of the sample populations is needed before the results are interpreted. All the following studies examined small manufacturing operations. They did not sample from the *Fortune 500*. Most of the organizations are of a size equal to a division in a multi-divisional firm. Some care should be taken, therefore, in generalizing to multi-divisional firms. Also, there is no examination of the departmental structure. The primary interest is in decentralization and in formalization of procedures.

The first study to appear was one by Negandhi and Reimann (1972). From a sample of thirty Indian manufacturing firms, they examined the relation between decentralization, performance, and the competitiveness of the industry. They measured performance on the basis of economic criteria (profit and sales growth) and behavioral criteria (for example morale, turnover, and interdepartmental relations). Their results are shown in Table 4.2. Decentralization is related to effectiveness under all conditions, but the strength of the relation varies with competitiveness. Under noncompetitive conditions, there is a weak relation between decentralization and performance. Thus, structure is important primarily under competitive conditions. This result is consistent with the prior interpretation of the effects of competition upon structure and performance. As always, care should be used in interpreting cause and effect in a cross-sectional study, as high performance could be the cause of decentralization. The important point here is the moderating effect of competition.

Table 4.2 Kendall's Correlation Coefficients for Decentralization Index vs Organization Effectiveness

Organization Effectiveness	Highly Competitive		Market Conditions Moderately Competitive		Noncompetitive	
(1) Behavioral criteria	0.80	(0.78) *	0.72	(0.69)	0.56	(0.56)
(2) Economic criteria	0.69	(0.66)	0.60 **	(0.52) ***	0.44	(0.48)

   * Coefficients in parentheses are Kendall's *partial* coefficients—organization size held constant.

   ** Not significant—all other correlations significant at 0.05 level (1-tail).

   *** No test of significance available for partial correlation coefficients.

From "A Contingency Theory of Organization Reexamined in the Context of a Developing Country," by Anant Negandhi and Bernard Reimann. Reprinted by permission.

Recently, the authors have reanalyzed the same data using statistical techniques that test for relations among groups of variables (Negandhi and Reimann 1976). Two relations emerged. The first was a relation between economic performance and competitiveness of the industry: the less the competition, the higher the economic performance. This result is consistent with the findings of economists (Bain 1958). If you have a monopoly, you do not need the coordination and control obtained through rational organization. The second relation that emerged was between the combination of economic and behavioral effectiveness, and two dimensions of structure—decentralization, and formalization or rationalization of decision procedures. The most effective organizations were the ones that decentralized and simultaneously evolved sophisticated processes for allocating resources. Competitiveness has less influence than structure upon behavioral criteria. The authors called the first relation short-run effectiveness and the latter long-run effectiveness.

The Negandhi-Reimann study has been replicated on a sample of Mexican and Italian manufacturing firms. Some of them are subsidiaries of American firms. The results shown in Table 4.3 are again consistent with prior interpretations of the effects of competition. Under conditions of competition, one finds a relation between structure and economic performance. The more decentralization under competitive conditions, the higher the economic performance. There is no relation between structure and performance under noncompetitive conditions. On behavioral measures, decentralization and effectiveness are positively related under all competitive conditions. Cause and effect still cannot be determined.

Table 4.3 Kendall's Correlation Coefficients: Decentralization vs. Organization Effectiveness

| | Market Conditions | | | |
| | High Competitive | | Low Competitive | |
Organization Effectiveness	Mexican	Italian	Mexican	Italian
Economic criteria	.60*	.39**	−.10	.00
Behavioral criteria	.71*	.38**	.51*	.69*

  * p < .05 level (1-tail)
 ** p < .10 level (1-tail)

From "A Contingency Theory of Organization Reexamined in the Context of a Developing Country," by Anant Negandhi and Bernard Reimann. Reprinted by permission.

A study by Khandwalla adds more support to the previous findings (1973). Using a sample of ninety-eight U.S. manufacturing firms, he measured industry competition, the amount of delegation of decision making, and the extent of the use of sophisticated management controls such as cost and variance analyses. His findings are that the greater the competition, the greater the use of controls and the greater the decentralization of decision making. The relations were strongest when competition was based on new products rather than on marketing or price. Again, decentralization is coupled with the use of formal control systems and is most extensive under competitive conditions.

The last study that will be reported here related competition, dimensions of structure and process, and various types of strategy and technology (Pfeffer and Leblebici 1973). They took their measures from a sample of thirty-eight small manufacturing firms. They found that the greater the competition, the greater the degree of specification of procedures (formalization) and the more frequent the reporting of results. These findings support the previous studies. The relation between decentralization and competition was again positive, but this time it was small and not statistically significant. In part, this result is attributable to the lack of control for economic effectiveness and to a different measure for decentralization (the amount of money a department head can spend without higher authorization).

The second part of the study examined relations between strategic variables such as number of product changes and structure and process variables. There is a mixture of results. Under competitive conditions, organizations reduce spans of control and add levels to the hierarchy; under noncompetitive conditions, organizations stay flat and increase spans of control and number of departments. Also, the greater the number of changes to products, the greater the formalization and written reporting of performance. The results for decentralization are mixed, with some positive results for competitive and some for noncompetitive conditions. In part, this could arise from a confounding with size as well as the previously mentioned economic performance. The larger the organization, the greater the amount of money a manager can spend without higher approval.

These results can be interpreted as being consistent with previous results. Greater competition brings on a need for greater coordination and control. The increase is obtained through the use of formalized systems and procedures for measuring and reporting performance and a greater delegation of decision making discretion within those systems and procedures. As a matter of fact, some current theorists argue that narrowing spans of control occur under uncertain conditions and are associated with decentralization (Perrow 1977). Under this interpretation, all the previous studies lead to the same results. Competitiveness affects organizational structure and process. The effects are decentralization and formalization. The more a firm is decentralized and formalized in a competitive environment, the stronger the relation with economic performance. The need for coordination and control is thus created in the competitive environment.

There is simply less need for coordination in noncompetitive conditions, and it is less important in order to obtain economic performance. These results support the view emerging from the studies of strategy and structure.

CONTINGENCY THEORY
AND PERFORMANCE

Several of the articles discussed above measured performance outcomes. In this section, we want to review that literature in its entirety. Recall the contingency hypothesis that the structure of the organization must fit the environment in which the firm is operating. If it does not, the firm should be less effective.

The hypothesis originated with the findings of Woodward and Lawrence and Lorsch. In both cases, the less effective firms deviated from the hypothesized fit with technology and environment. A number of subsequent studies have confirmed that relation, although two have not.

Lorsch and his colleagues have twice replicated his original results. As reported earlier in the chapter, a study of corporate divisional relations demonstrated that low performers deviated from the optimal fit, and high performers did not (Lorsch and Allen 1973). In another study to be described later, he found that high performers on routine tasks had mechanistic organizations, and high performers on nonroutine tasks had organic structures (Lorsch and Morse 1975). The low performers had mechanistic structures for nonroutine tasks and organic structures for routine ones.

Khandwalla attempted to replicate the Woodward results (1974). Using a scale that measured the degree to which a firm used mass production or continuous process techniques, he predicted that mass and continuous production would be associated with the acquisition of prior and subsequent operations in the work flow, delegation of authority, and coordination through sophisticated control systems. In general, the hypotheses held, but it was the high performers that conformed more to the hypothesis than the low performers. Again, the high performers achieved a better fit.

Child has examined structure and performance in six industries in Britain (1974, 1975). He was interested in the effects of size and dynamic environments on the degree to which firms acquired formal controls and staff specialists, and delegated authority. Increases in each are referred to as the degree of bureaucratization. The high performing firms acquired bureaucracy at a faster rate when they grew than did the poor performers. With size should come bureaucracy. Although the high performers in dynamic environments acquired bureaucracy at a slower rate than the high performers in stable industries, they did so faster than low performers in both environments. In a dynamic environment, a balance must be struck between bureaucracy for size and responsiveness for change. Again, the notion is one of fit.

The studies in the previous section should also be cited here. Neghandhi and Reimann (1973) and Simonetti and Boseman (1975) both found that in competitive environments, decentralization led to high performance. Presumably, operations need to be decentralized in more dynamic competitive situations in order to fit with the environment. Here again is the usual caution about cause and effect when interpreting performance-decentralization relations.

These studies all support the fit hypothesis. However, several problems are present. First is the notion of causation. It is not clear whether low performance causes centralization, or vice versa. Decentralization is always one of the structural variables used. Second, the importance of structure is not clear. There appears to be a relation between structure and performance, but it may be weak or strong. The earlier Poensgen and Cable and Speer studies give us some idea of this relationship, but there is no analysis of variance among the contingency studies.

Finally, there are two studies that do not report results to support the fit hypothesis. In both cases, there was no support for a direct test that organic or decentralized organizations perform better than centralized organizations in uncertain environments (Mohr 1971; Pennings 1975). Both studies have experimental holes of their own, primarily because their sample was taken from a single context. Therefore, there was a restricted range of variation. However, the studies do give cause for skepticism and for avoiding too hasty an adoption of simple contingency relations.

SUMMARY

This chapter reviewed studies not directly motivated by Chandler which provide a more intensive look at the processes within an organization.

Galbraith's Boeing study provides an example of the strategy-structure-competition "fit" hypothesis. Given a monopoly position and product leadership, Boeing was not pressed by time constraints. It was able to manage its projects through a functional structure. However, when competition became a crucial factor and the number of markets enlarged, Boeing had to reorganize into a divisional form.

An important distinction is made in this chapter between structures that at first glance appear similar but actually differ in their *degree* of centralization and in the actual processes within the firm. For example, Berg differentiates between diversified majors and conglomerates. The diversified majors were the multi-divisional type of form described by Chandler, which usually had several hundred people in the corporate office. They coordinated divisional activity through corporate policy and direct participation of corporate offices. The conglomerate, on the other hand, which is similar to the holding company form, usually had only ten to twenty people in the corporate office. They placed nearly all functions within the division and eliminated the need for coordination. Here, the corporate divisional interests were coordinated through the reward system.

Diversified majors and conglomerates were seen as corresponding to the strategies of diversification into related businesses and unrelated businesses, respectively. This was apparently a logical fit, because the relatedness caused a need for more coordination, whereas the unrelated businesses created less need for integration and could be operated independently. This fit was then tested by Lawrence and Lorsch, who found that the firms having a proper fit performed at a higher level than firms that did not. Their conclusion was that strategies characterized by diversity and uncertainty required greater decentralization and self-containment of divisions. When autonomy is not given, however, lower performance results.

The above findings constitute what organization theorists call a contingency theory. The theory states that there is no one best way of organizing, but that all ways of organizing are not equally effective. That is, the choice of organization form makes a difference in economic performance. The choice depends, however, on the situation.

Organizational contingency theorists, such as Burns and Stalker and Lawrence and Lorsch, suggest that the rate of change in the environment determines organization form. They say that successful organizations in industries with high rates of change of markets and technology adopt an organic form characterized by decentralization, ambiguous roles, and extensive lateral communication. A mechanistic form characterized by centralization, well defined roles, and communication following a chain of command was adopted by successful firms encountering stable markets and product lines.   These results once again lend support to Chandler's thesis.

Thus far, we have discussed the concept of the strategy-structure fit and its relation to economic performance.   We have not, however, discussed precisely how organizations engaged in many diverse activities can coordinate these activities in such a way as to form an integrated whole.   That is the task of our next chapter.

5

Strategy, Mechanisms of Integration, and Integrating Roles

In this chapter we shall take a look at coordination mechanisms used to cope with general management problems associated with various product-market strategies.

Organizations have created a number of information sharing and decision making processes to integrate or coordinate activities, particularly those activities that cut across divisional and departmental boundaries. These processes vary from simple spontaneous meetings to complicated matrix forms. Our task here is to identify these processes, to order them in a way that will allow them to be related to strategy, and to identify the conditions under which the different processes should be chosen for implementing strategy.

INTEGRATION MECHANISMS

Organization theorists had occasionally performed studies that examined interdepartmental contact and communication. However, the results were not very operational, because it was not clear what were the mechanisms that produced the contact. The Lawrence and Lorsch work made a significant step toward giving us a language for talking about these lateral processes. They postulated two dimensions that were important for organizational effectiveness. First, organizations had to differentiate their functions so that each functional department could deal with its different subenvironment. Second, it had to integrate the differentiated functions around the interdependencies brought on by the key competitive requirements of the industry. For those firms where new product introduction was the key competitive issue, the integration problem was one of coordinating marketing and research and development. Where on-time delivery was the key competitive issue, the integration problem was one of coordinating marketing and production. The Lawrence and Lorsch thesis was that the most effective firms would be those that had differentiated their functions to the extent needed to adapt to functional subenvironments and had simultaneously found mechanisms to integrate the differentiated functions in order to deal with the competitive issue of the overall corporate environment. The results for the mechanisms of integration are shown in Table 5.1.

Table 5.1 Integrating Mechanisms Used in Three Different Industries

	Plastics	Food	Container
% New products in last 20 years	35%	15%	0%
Integrating devices	Rules	Rules	Rules
	Hierarchy	Hierarchy	Hierarchy
	Goal setting	Goal setting	Goal setting
	Direct contact	Direct contact	Direct contact
	Teams at 3 levels	Task forces	
	Integrating Dept.	Integrators	
% Integrators/ managers	22%	17%	0%

The Table shows the integration mechanisms used by the *most effective* firms in three different industries. That is, the Table shows the variation across industries, as exhibited by those firms that have successfully adapted to that industry. There are two main implications of this Table. (For more extensive discussion, *see* Galbraith 1973). First, the Table shows the different kinds of mechanisms used to integrate interdepartmental activities. Four of the mechanisms are used by all the firms. The hierarchy of authority is the principal mechanism used to resolve interdepartmental problems. The problem is referred upward into the hierarchy to a common superior who oversees all departments affected by the problem. When a problem arises frequently, a rule or procedure is devised for it as a substitute for hierarchical referral. Other problems are best solved on the spot, so goals are set by way of planning processes like scheduling and budgeting. Organizational control shifts from control over behavior to control over results, and discretion over actions to achieve results is decentralized. Exceptions to goals and rules are either referred to the hierarchy, or are resolved on the spot through direct contact between affected parties. The informal, spontaneous processes serve as another substitute for hierarchical referral. These four processes constitute standard practice for all three industries.

The second feature illustrated in Table 5.1 is the requirement of some firms for more mechanisms for coordination. The food processing firms and plastics firms need more than the standard practices, for example. In contrast to the effective container firm, they have evolved cross-functional teams and task forces to manage the activity associated with the introduction of new products. These group mechanisms are actually substitutes for the general manager. The general manager would make these decisions under less variable and less diverse conditions. Also, new roles were created to help integrate the cross-departmental new product activities. Product managers were created to cope with diverse product lines and new product creation. These too are general manager equivalents. Pieces of general management work needed to coordinate interfunctional work when introducing new products are delegated to groups and integrating roles. But this delegation occurs only under conditions of diversity and uncertainty. The added managerial effort was not needed for the more predictable and less diverse container industry.

In summary, there are a number of specific mechanisms that are used to achieve interdepartmental coordination. These mechanisms vary from hierarchical referral to the addition of integrating departments such as product management departments. An enlarged list of mechanisms is shown below:

- —Hierarchy
- —Rules
- —Goal Setting (Planning)
- —Direct Contact
- —Interdepartmental Liaison Roles
- —Temporary Task Forces
- —Permanent Teams
- —Integrating Roles
- —Integrating Departments

Organizations select from the list those mechanisms that will permit them to implement their strategy. The selection is not random, however; choice makes a difference.

The list of coordination mechanisms is an ordered list. Each step down the list represents the commitment to a more complicated and more expensive mechanism of coordination. The increasing expenditure of resources for coordination results, first, because integrating departments are more expensive than temporary task forces using line managers. But expenditures increase also, because mechanisms at the bottom of the list are added to, not substituted for, those high on the list. They are not direct substitutes. The plastics organization uses all coordination mechanisms. Therefore, an organization should select from the list starting at the top and going down only as far as is necessary in order to implement its strategy. The successful container firm stopped at direct contact, the successful food processor stopped with integrators (product managers), and the plastics firm adopted all of them in order to be successful. The costs of these mechanisms can be seen by comparing the percentage of managers who play integrating, as opposed to line, roles. These figures are shown at the bottom of the Table. In the plastics organization, twenty-two percent of the managers work in product management activities, yet they have a functional organization. In contrast, the container firm has no managers working in integrating roles. The difference is attributable to the amount of new product introduction that must be undertaken to remain competitive in the industry, and the level of technology required to support the new products. The more new product activity, the higher the level of technology and uncertainty the more the hierarchy needs to be buttressed with cross-departmental coordination mechanisms. Therefore, those organizations pursuing strategies characterized by interdepartmental activity, high uncertainty, and high diversity will select mechanisms farther down on the list than those organizations pursuing strategies characterized by low uncertainty and diversity.

The hypothesis that strategies characterized by uncertainty and diversity lead to cross-departmental processes (teams) and integrating roles is supported and elaborated by the work of Corey and Star (1971). They studied various types and responsibilities of integrating roles (program structures, in their terminology) in functional business structures. First, they identified more complex integrating role combinations. For example, they showed the Monsanto Organic Chem-

Figure 5.1 Monsanto Organic Chemicals Division 1963 Illustrating Product Management Directorates and Functional Organization

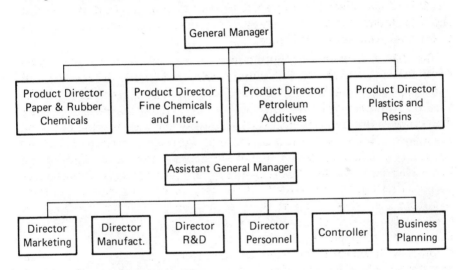

SOURCE: Corey and Star 1971, p. 346.

icals Division structure (1967) as illustrating the type of integrating role that characterized the Lawrence and Lorsch plastics firms. The chart is shown in Figure 5.1. It illustrates product management departments (directorates), which are overlaid on a basic functional structure. This structure is a response to product diversification strategies designed when size limits the creation of multi-divisional structures, sometimes in the presence of significant economies of scale in one or more functions as well. However, they also note that some organizations experience diversity in markets as well as in products. Some organizations then adopted market based integrating departments. An example was IBM meeting the need to tailor the same product lines to government and commercial markets and to distinguish between manufacturing, retailing, and banking submarket applications within commercial markets. And, finally, they presented some organizations like IBM and Du Pont, who have experienced both market and product diversity. The response of these organizations has been to organize simultaneously by markets, products, and functions. The Du Pont Fibers organization of 1956 is shown in Figure 5.2. The integrating departments are located in marketing in order to coordinate with the regional sales force and to take a marketing focus. The geographic sales force is concerned with the short-run approach to clients in their area. The industry market groups are concerned with intermediate-term issues such as market strategy, forecasts, promotions, and coordination with field sales. The product managers are concerned with longer-run issues of product strategy, new product development, product scheduling, and coordination with manufacturing and research. Thus, diversity is handled within functional organizations by developing integrating roles around the sources of diversity.

The second point made by Corey and Star was that the greater the diversity and the greater the amount of new product introduction, the greater the likelihood of integrating roles and departments and the greater was their influence. Thus, integrating roles represents one of the principal means with which to implement diversification strategies *without reorganizing* into a product divisionalized structure.

In summary, it has been shown that organizations create integrating mechnisms in order to cope with general management problems of interdepartmental coordination caused by product and market diversity. The mechanisms, such as product task forces, are information and decision processes that are general manager substitutes but are less than full-time equivalents that result from product divisionalized structures. These mechanisms vary in their cost and their ability to cope with uncertainty and diversity. The more diversity in the business strategy, the greater the number of mechanisms adopted. For diverse and uncertain strategies, separate roles are created around the sources of diversity. These roles, such as product management roles, represent the move to simultaneous structures, which are structures in which the organization is simultaneously product and functional, or any other combination.

Figure 5.2 Du Pont Fibers Organization 1956 Showing Industrial Market and Product Integrating Departments

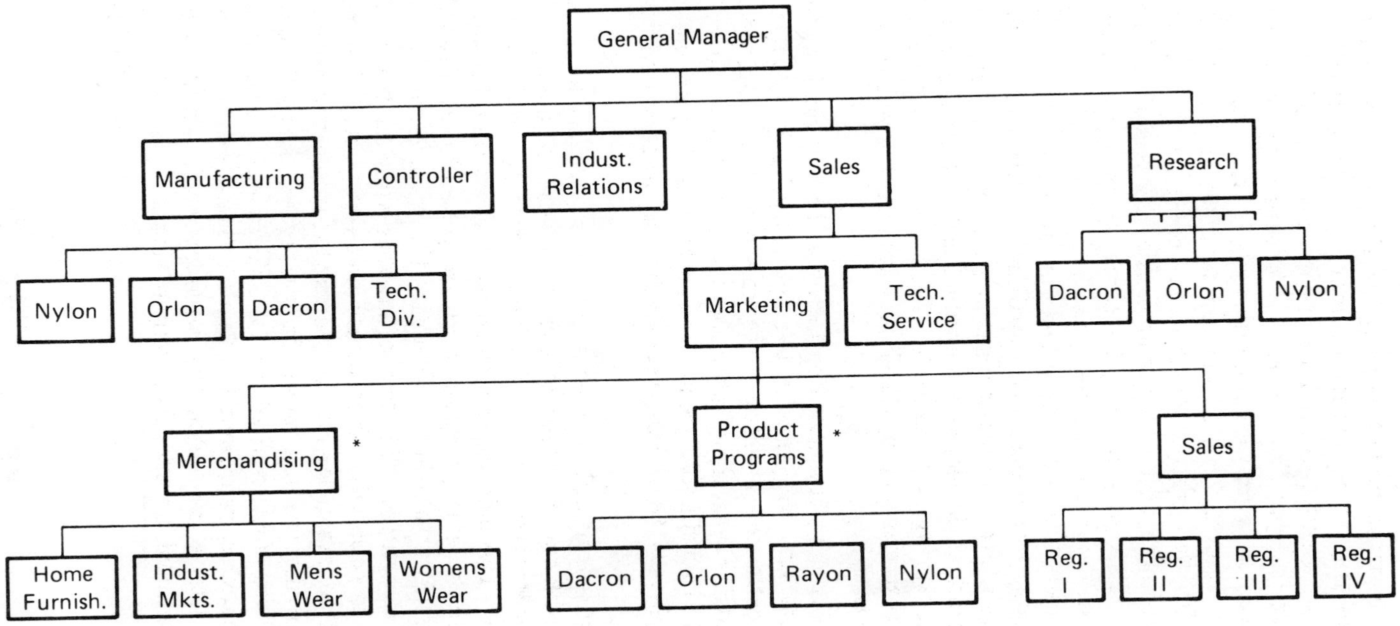

Figure 5.3 The Range of Alternatives

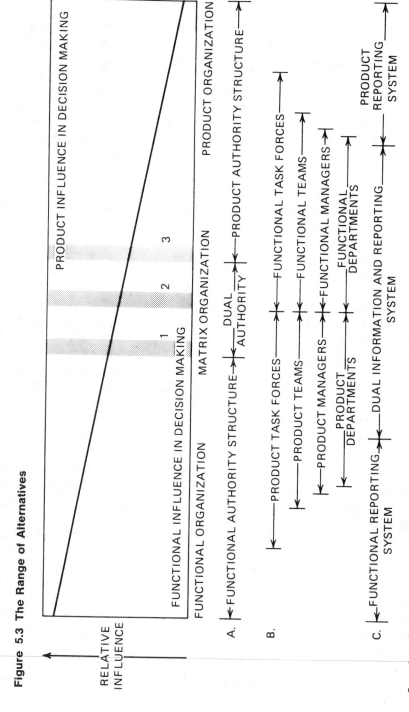

SIMULTANEOUS
OR MATRIX STRUCTURES

The adoption of coordination mechanisms with which functional organizations can manage diversity suggests that there are a number of transition phases between the functional and multi-divisional structures. Indeed, each step down the list of coordination mechanisms represents a step toward more product oriented decision making. Thus, the change from functional to product structures need not be a major discrete alteration but can be an evolutionary movement. There is a continuous range of distribution of influence between product and functional orientations. This description is shown in Figure 5.3.

One moves along the distribution of influence by adding additional coordination mechanisms and adding power to integrating roles. The point at which product and function are of equal power is called the matrix organization. At that point, there are simultaneously two line organizations of equal power. The organization is simultaneously functional and product. Equal power is obtained through multiple authority relations. The chart for such a company is shown in Figure 5.4. It shows a matrix organization for a geographically organized bank that is pursuing a strategy of segmenting markets and creating new financial services for those markets. The resulting market diversity forces the bank into a simultaneous structure built around markets and geography. At some point, the two structures must intersect. In Figure 5.4 the market organization and geographic organization intersect at the country level. The individual who manages multi-national corporate banking has two bosses—the country manager and the market manager. The task of that individual is to integrate the two perspectives for that business in that country.

One could also move to the right-hand side of the diagram in Figure 5.3 where the product divisions are dominant and the functional managers play integrating roles. This form was the one adopted by the Commercial Airplane Division of Boeing, whose story was told above. Thus, organizers are not faced with a choice of function versus product (or market or geography) divisions, but with a choice of whether to give priority to product or function. Organizations nowadays are simultaneous structures (simply a generalization of line staff models), with product and functional managers reporting to the general manager. Multi-national firms add a third geographic dimension. Which dimension is more influential and has higher priority depends upon several factors, including the strategy and the business environment.

Several factors favor emphasizing the product side. As already mentioned, diversity and new product introductions are best managed

Figure 5.4 Worldwide Matrix for a Banking Firm

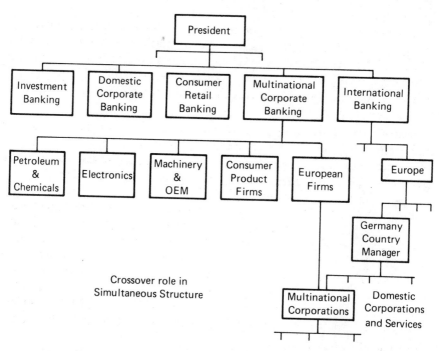

through product oriented structures. One would move to the right of the diagram as a result. Also, increasing interdependence among functional departments and increased need for responsiveness to the market favor a product or project orientation. However, these generalizations must be qualified by considerations of size. Self-contained product divisions may be too small to have their own sales force or to achieve size economies in production. Therefore, the larger the organization, the more likely the establishment of product or project divisions. The smaller the organization, the more likely the establishment of product or project integrating departments. The longer the life cycle of the product or project, the more likely it is that a self-contained division will be created.

A couple of factors favor the functional organization. Economies of scale in the functions mitigate against breaking them up and distributing the pieces among the product divisions. The need for special expertise and career paths for specialists are facilitated by the functional form. Therefore, firms pursuing state-of-the-art technology should have strong technical functions. The uncertainty connected with high technology also argues for a coordination capability across functions. It is usually the high technology firms that adopt some form of the matrix, which simultaneously gives them high technology and high coordination.

The general business environment also influences the organization's strategy. Galbraith describes how the business environment has shifted in the aerospace industry and how organization structures have been adopted in order for the firms to remain competitive. These changes are independent of considerations based on size, product diversity, technology, and so on.

In the late 1950s and early 1960s, technical performance was the critical dimension. The environment was characterized by Sputnik, the space race, and the missile gap. It was deemed imperative by the government to produce technical accomplishments and to do so rapidly. The priorities placed technical performance first, schedule second, and cost a poor third. Data on actual performance during this time period reflect this order of priorities. All projects met or exceeded technical specifications, but completion times were 1.5 times as great as projected, and costs exceeded targets by a factor of 3.2. In aerospace firms performing these projects, the functional managers dominated the joint decisions, but project managers were also influential because of time pressures. Since technical performance dominated other considerations, the influence distribution was approximated by the dotted line (1) in Figure 5.3.

In the early and middle 1960s, the environment changed. This was the McNamara era. McNamara believed that technical performance could be achieved, but at less cost. The contracts changed from cost plus fixed fee to various incentive contracts and fixed price contracts. Defense Department officials demanded that aerospace firms use PERT, then PERT/Cost information systems. The effect of these changes was to make the project manager more influential in the decision process. In Figure 5.3 the influence distribution was represented by the dotted line (2).

Still another change occurred in the late 1960s. Strong pressures to reduce defense costs began to operate. First, there was the publicity concerning cost overruns on the giant C–5A aircraft. Senator Proxmire began hearings on contractor efficiency practices. Finally, inflation and shifting national priorities combined to make cost the top priority, as opposed to technical performance and schedule completion. In the internal workings of aerospace firms, the project managers began to dominate the joint decision processes. The pattern of influence was explicit. Project managers held vice-presidential status, whereas laboratory and functional managers had the title of "director." The influence distribution moved to line (3) in Figure 5.3.

Currently, still another change is occurring. The national government is shifting spending away from aerospace projects. The effect is to reduce the size of the aerospace industry and of firms in it. The firms must retain specialized personnel to create the technology while meeting demands to reduce costs and size. Thus, the effective utilization of specialized resources across a number of projects has increased in importance. Firms must avoid duplication of personnel or fractional utilization of shared resources. Internally, the need to increase utilization is causing the functional managers to regain some of their previous strengths. Reduced size increased the importance of the utilization of resources and of its champion, the resource manager.

This brief account of the aerospace industry demonstrates the effect of environmental influences upon internal decision processes. Normally, the general manager would watch these trends and alter decision making behavior accordingly. When decisions are decentralized, however, the general managers must change internal power bases as well as their own decision behavior. It becomes the task of the general manager to see that the distribution of internal influence reflects the external realities faced by the organization. The general manager must therefore take an open system view of the organization (Galbraith 1973, pp. 117–118).

Several implications can be derived from the scenario. First, the matrix is not the ultimate structure but, like all structures, is a transitional one that should be adopted when conditions merit and discarded when conditions no longer pertain. Second, simultaneous structures are flexible structures that can be adjusted and fine tuned by altering the power distribution of the existing roles as strategy and environment change. There is less need for the wrenching reorganization of GM described by Chandler. Third, the task of the chief executive is one of power balancing. The power balance among the roles needs to be adjusted continually with regard to assignments, salary, physical location, titles, and other factors. Thus, as technological changes such as minicomputers reduce economies of scale and promote power shifts to self-contained product divisions, the chief executive needs to plan the organization as he or she plans strategy and investments. The internal power distribution must produce decisions consistent with external reality and strategy.

SUMMARY

In this chapter we were concerned with the coordinating mechanisms used to cope with general management problems that are associated with various product-market strategies. This is an important issue, because, as Lawrence and Lorsch point out, the most effective firms are those that differentiate their functions to the extent needed to adapt to functional subenvironments, while simultaneously finding mechanisms to integrate these differentiated functions. These integrating mechanisms provide a means of dealing with issues relating to the overall corporate environment.

There are a number of specific mechanisms, then, that are used to achieve this interdepartmental coordination. They range from hierarchical referral to the creation of product management departments. These mechanisms increase in cost and also in their ability to cope with uncertainty and diversity as one moves toward the product management departments. The organization must choose from this ordered list of mechanisms.

Organizations pursuing strategies characterized by interdepartmental activity, high uncertainty, and high diversity will select mechanisms further down the list (closer to integrating departments) than organizations pursuing strategies characterized by low uncertainty and diversity.

Also, each step down the list of coordinating mechanisms represents a step toward a more product oriented structure. Therefore, the change from a functional to a product structure need not be a major discrete alteration but can be an evolutionary movement. The point at which product and function are of equal power is called a matrix organization. The choice for the organizer becomes whether to give priority to product or to function. Factors favoring a move to the product side include diversity, new product introductions, increasing interdependence among functional departments, and an increased need for responsiveness to markets. However, the organization must be large enough to achieve economies of scale in production. The factors that favor remaining with a functional organization include the economy of scale factor, the need for special expertise, and the need for career paths for specialists.

The next chapter presents studies that describe the actual processes and systems within an organization and shows how they vary according to variations in strategy and structure.

6

Systems and Processes for Managing Diversity

The phenomena that constitute organizations are not only structural in nature. There are other phenomena such as resource allocation processes, performance evaluation and reward systems, integrating mechanisms, and many others, all of which constitute the form of the organization. This section reviews the relevant research analyzing the relationship of strategy to these processes.

The importance of these other phenomena was noticed by Chandler. In discussing the General Motors case, he spent a great deal of time discussing the invention of accounting practices, such as standard volume and other performance measurement and reporting systems; the implementation and linkage of interdivisional committees; the creation of new roles, such as the group executive; and the difference in the personality between managers who invented the strategy and those who invented the structure. In this chapter we examine what has been done in these categories since his work. First, we will examine resource allocation processes, then performance evaluation and reward systems, and finally the human issues of career and management development.

RESOURCE ALLOCATION PROCESSES

Organizations undertake a myriad of activities in allocating their resources. These activities are usually labeled as budgeting and planning and control processes. These are the processes that Rumelt and Williamson suggested were responsible for the superior performance of the multi-divisional firm in managing diversity. Although a great deal of scholarly attention has been devoted to methods of allocating resources rationally from an economic viewpoint, much less attention has been given to examining the decisions as organizational and political processes. There are a few exceptions, however, and these studies provide a good base for further exploration. Most of the studies are of a general descriptive nature, but some compare process differences based upon differences in strategy or structure.

Some of the studies use Cyert and March's *Behavioral Theory of the Firm* as their point of departure (1963). The behavioral theory was intended to introduce a better description of how decisions actually were made rather than how they should be made. They indicate that if one introduces cognitive limits of human beings, together with uncertainty and lack of agreement over goals, then the actual processes are quite different from those prescribed by management scientists. Their work prompted others to view resource allocation not as single choices but as organizational processes. For instance, it is very difficult to determine who made a decision or when a decision was made.

Aharoni found that

> there is no one investment decision made at a specific point in time. Rather, it is a long *process*, spread over a considerable period of time and involving many people at different echelons of various organizations. Throughout this process numerous "subdecisions" have to be made. These "subdecisions" usually reduce the degree of freedom of the decision making unit and therefore influence the final outcome of the process (1966, p. 35).

Another study that illustrates how the processes in an organization actually differ from the rational economic model is one done by Carter. He showed how strategy affected decisions and confirmed the lack of analysis in decision making. The decision to invest is made by someone in the organization, then the information is collected and analyses performed to tailor the request to the interests of top management and the chosen strategy.

The last general descriptive study to be mentioned here is the specific examination of the resource allocation process in a large diversified company by Bower (1970). He distinguished three sequential steps that took place at three different levels of the organization. First, was the *definition* phase at the division level, where a need for investment was recognized and a proposal created to reduce a discrepancy. Next, the proposal was given *impetus* when a division manager bought it and agreed to back it and commit himself to it. Finally, there was the *approval* by corporate management in the allocating of scarce funds. His work is a thorough description of this process for four investments. He too was interested in describing the actual process and in distinguishing it from more quantitative but naive versions of investment decisions. No attempt was made by Bower or the other researchers mentioned above to distinguish variations in the process and to relate them to variations in strategy.

Subsequent work has introduced variations in process that accompany variations in structure and strategy. Ackerman used the Bower model to compare paper manufacturing divisions in two integrated paper companies and in two diversified multi-divisional firms. Holding industry constant, he assigned variations in process to variations in structure. The result, as referred to earlier, was greater centralization of the defintion and impetus stages in the vertically integrated company. The results are represented schematically in Figure 6.1.

Figure 6.1 Organization Levels and the Investment Process

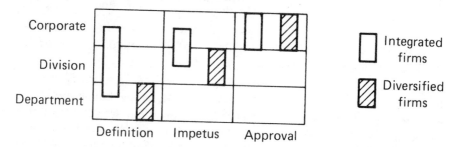

SOURCE: Ackerman 1971, p. 350.

In the integrated companies, all three levels are active in the definition phase of new investments and often suggest the need for new investments. In the diversified company, all investment proposals were initiated by the department level. During the impetus phase, corporate mangement made their own analysis of risk, and the diversified firms left that task to the division. Similarly, there was a great deal of personal interaction between division and corporate levels during the analysis in the integrated firm, whereas the diversified firms again relied on the division manager, using selection of the manager and subsequent accountability for performance as the means of control. The diversified firm viewed the budget numbers as a contract to which the division was committed. The integrated companies did not, since the corporate level had much to do with the decision. Thus, the integrated firm adopted a centralized process for allocating capital in its vertically integrated, interdependent firm. The diversified firms behaved as did the firm in Bower's original work. These findings are quite consistent with those of Lorsch and Allen, reported earlier, which took a more aggregate view in examining all decision processes. Lorsch and Allen found a more active corporate unit in more areas of decision making in the integrated firms. In addition, their measurement of performance allowed them to suggest that the process is an appropriate one.

The work of Berg provides another comparative study. His approach was to contrast the conglomerate with the more standard multi-divisional form. The conglomerates usually pursue even more diverse strategies than the multi-divisional. The resource allocation processes are even more decentralized than those described by Ackerman. However, they did use a few sophisticated financial planning and control information systems. From Berg's study, one gets the impression that the modern conglomerate finds companies that need better management, acquires them, and turns them around. The turnaround is accomplished by a corporate group skilled in general management that acts like a consulting firm with ownership clout. Many of the reasons for the success of these organizations and their processes is attributable to their growth by acquisition rather than by internal development; they seek businesses with no relationship, instead of exploiting a distinctive functional competence.

Pitts (1977) has outlined some of the differences between firms that pursue internal diversification strategies and those that diversify by acquisition. The internal diversifier is characterized by larger corporate staffs, more interdivisional transfers, a more subjective performance appraisal, and, in short, more interdivisional sharing of resources. The internal diversifier, then, actively exploits opportunities for resource sharing; the acquisitive diversifier deliberately foregoes such opportunities. The main strength of the internal diversifier is that it brings to a new business its ability to draw upon the combined resources of its numerous dimensions, especially in the technological area. On the other hand, the key capability of the acquisitive diversifier rests in its ability to attract and retain acquired managers who themselves possess expertise in newly entered fields. They are then given high division autonomy, financial backing, general management coaching, and performance targets. Pitts points out that, because of the fundamental differences between the two strategies, any attempt to define a compromise position somewhere between the two might very well prove disastrous.

The last study to be discussed is the work of Oliver Williamson (1976). He has explicitly contrasted the functional form with the multi-divisional form in managing large and diverse enterprises. He is more interested in the outcomes of resource allocation than in the process, however. His argument is based partly on the hypothesis that additional hierarchical levels in functional organizations cause a loss of control and a reduction of profit maximizing behavior. In oligopolistic industries, the lack of product-market competition allows this behavior to persist. However, the formation of independent "natural" business units in the multi-divisional form creates units for which profit can be measured and across which funds can be transferred. The multi-divisional form can identify and audit substandard performance and remove inferior management more easily than the capital market could if the units operated independently. These measurement and audit features lead Williamson to propose that resources are more likely to be used optimally (profit maximizing) in the multi-divisional firm when it is faced with large and diverse businesses.

In summary, progress has been made in developing an understanding of processes by which organizations allocate strategic resources. Some progress has also been made in creating a language for discussing and comparing these different processes. A few studies have found variations in process to be related to different strategies. One study and a conceptual argument suggest that these variations lead to more effective economic performance. One of the reasons that resources are effectively allocated is that evaluation and reward systems are tied to planned resource usage.

Figure 6.2 Strategy, Structure, and Processes

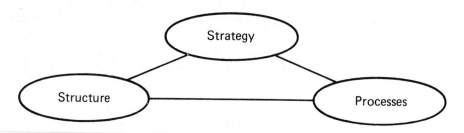

EVALUATION AND REWARD SYSTEMS

One of the most important components of an organization form is the reward system by which performance is measured, evaluated, and rewarded. The study of rewards and punishments from a motivational view has been a major research area for organization behavior specialists. Most of this work has been directed at testing various models of motivation, at questions of whether extrinsic or intrinsic rewards are more motivating, and at examining various policies to make work more satisfying. Much of the work also concentrates on lower and middle level personnel. The best recent work summarizing research on reward systems, and compensation in particular, is that of Lawler (1971, 1977). Lawler suggests that the research confirms the conventional wisdom that when pay is tied to performance, it motivates higher performance. But despite its obviousness, this is not a unanimous view (Meyer 1975).

Lawler's work has also led to a typology of the different kinds of pay plans and their likely motivational consequences. First, money rewards can be given as salary increases or bonuses. The reward can be given on the basis of individual, group, or organization-wide performance. Secondly, performance can be measured by productivity or profit, by cost effectiveness or cost reduction, or by superior's rating. Lawler rates these pay plans according to their ability to tie pay to performance, to produce dysfunctional side effects (such as encouraging short-run performance at long-run expense), to encourage cooperative behavior between people, and to promote employee acceptance. The results are shown in Table 6.1.

The ratings are from 1 to 5. The higher the number, the stronger the relation. Thus, individual bonuses based on productivity or profit are best at linking pay and performance but have the strongest relation to side effects and are weakest at encouraging cooperation. Several tradeoffs are evident. If a manager wants to reduce side effects, he or she does so at the expense of the pay-performance-individual initiative relation. The more one opts for global and cooperative plans, the more ambiguous the individual "pay for performance relation." The last point raised by Lawler is the concept of system congruence. That is, there is no single best reward system. The best depends on the organization's task and strategy, and on the fit of the reward system with the organization's structure, processes, and other systems.

The linkage between compensation policy and strategy has been considered and elaborated by Salter (1973). When considering incentive

Table 6.1 Ratings of Various Pay Incentive Plans

		Tie Pay to Per-formance	Produce Negative Side Effects	Encourage Coopera-tion	Employee Accept-ance
Salary Reward					
Individual plan	Productivity	4	1	1	4
	Cost effectiveness	3	1	1	4
	Superiors' rating	3	1	1	3
Group	Productivity	3	1	2	4
	Cost effectiveness	3	1	2	4
	Superiors' rating	2	1	2	3
Organization-wide	Productivity	2	1	3	4
	Cost effectiveness	2	1	2	4
Bonus					
Individual plan	Productivity	5	3	1	2
	Cost effectiveness	4	2	1	2
	Superiors' rating	4	2	1	2
Group	Productivity	4	1	3	3
	Cost effectiveness	3	1	3	3
	Superiors' rating	3	1	3	3
Organization-wide	Productivity	3	1	3	4
	Cost effectiveness	3	1	3	4
	Profit	2	1	3	3

or bonus compensation for group and division executives, several choices are available. First, there is a choice of financial instruments such as cash, stock, deferred cash, and several others. Second, there is the choice of performance measure and the amount of discretion in allocating the rewards. Finally, the amount of bonus is considered. In choosing a plan, Salter suggests that management analyze the strategy in order to examine the time horizon of the decision maker (short-run vs. long-run), the amount of risk taking to encourage the degree of cooperation with other managers that is required, and the likely differences between corporate and division goals. The results of his analysis are shown in Table 6.2. His recommendations, which are generally consistent with those of Lawler, give management some basis for designing reward policies.

Several examples can be given of the use of these policies. The incentive package at Boeing following the mid-1960s reorganization had

Table 6.2 Key Aspects of Incentive Compensation

Policy issues	Financial instruments	Performance measures	Degree of discretion in allocating bonus awards	Size & frequency of awards
Short-run vs. long-run	Mix of current bonus awards and stock options should reflect the relevant time horizon for policy-level executives. Deferred instruments are weak reinforcers of short-term performance.	Mix of quantitative measures of performance and more qualitative measures should reflect the relevant time horizon for executives. Qualitative measures usually reflect long-run considerations more effectively than quantitative measures.	Nondiscretionary, formula-based bonuses tend to encourage a short-run point of view.	Frequent bonus awards encourage concentration on short-term performance.
Risk aversion vs. risk taking	Current bonus awards, in cash or stock, can reinforce risk-taking behavior.	Qualitative measures of performance can reinforce initiative by assuring executives that total performance will be evaluated for purposes of bonus awards.	Completely discretionary, highly personalized bonuses do not clarify the "rules of the game" and as a result can discourage risk-taking behavior.	The size of both salary and incentive awards should be commensurate with the business and personal risks involved.
Interdivisional relationships		Bonus pools can be based on divisional performance, total corporate performance, or some mix of the two. Each arrangement sends different signals in terms of interdivisional cooperation.	Nondiscretionary, formula-based bonuses for division managers are most practical in companies where little cooperation among divisions is required. Discretionary bonuses are practical when top management wants to encourage cooperation among divisions.	
Company-division relationships	Stock options can effectively link the interests of division personnel to the interests of the corporation.	Use of objective measures of performance for division managers is more meaningful where the primary role of headquarters is to allocate capital than it is in instances where the head office plays an important role in "managing the business" of the divisions.	Nondiscretionary, formula-based bonuses are most practical in companies where headquarters does not interfere in management of the profit centers. Discretionary bonuses are mort useful when top management wants to exert a direct influence on decisions in the divisions.	

From Malcolm S. Salter, "Tailor Incentive Compensation to Strategy," *Harvard Business Review,* March–April 1973, Copyright © 1973 by the President and Fellows of Harvard College; all rights reserved.

several components to it. About 50 percent of the compensation package was bonus determined. One-third resulted from the negotiated profit target of the manager's program (707 or 747), and another third resulted from the profit of the Commercial Airplane Division as a whole. This was added to encourage the sharing of technical ideas across programs and to encourage cooperation in sharing technical and managerial talent and common customers. And finally, the last third resulted from a technological audit to determine the program's contribution to the company's technical base. The policy encourages risk taking (50 percent bonus), interprogram cooperation, individual performance, and long-run technical consideration. Other firms focus on group executives and compensate them on varying proportions of company versus group profit.

There is a trend toward greater use of total corporate profit rather than group or division profit in determining bonuses. In part the trend is the result of greater use of some form of matrix organization. There is a greater need to think in terms of the organization as a whole and to generate cooperation across units. One firm gives a bonus which is about half of the group executive's total compensation. The amount is determined 50 percent by the group's profit and 50 percent by the total company profit. In return, the group executive is to spend half time on the management committee and half time on internal group affairs. In this way the group executive who manages the cash-generating division ("cash cow") is more willing to see investments shifted to the cash user ("star"), which has a greater return or growth potential.

In summary, the Lawler and the Salter schemes require that the reward system designer start with the strategy of the organization, in order to determine the behavior that is necessary for implementation of that strategy. They identify some types for us, such as degree of cooperation between units and need for goal congruence between successive layers. The reward system chosen will be a trade-off between the various incentives for particular behaviors. A typical trade-off is between division profit incentives and total corporate profit. The total figure will encourage cooperation and congruence between division and corporate goals, but will reduce the degree to which an individual's performance is linked to his or her bonus. A balanced incentive scheme should be formulated according to the strategy, the interdependence between units, and the individualism of the managers in question.

A few of the research studies mentioned earlier also have compared reward system variation with strategy and structure variation. Berg credits the conglomerate with motivating managers rather than coordinating them (1969). The interdependence and need for co-operation between divisions is eliminated, and managers are rewarded generously on the basis of financial performance, usually with equity compensation. Thus, they are encouraged to take risks, to take a short- and long-term view, and to balance division versus corporate goals. Cooperation is voluntary and encouraged only if it pays off for the division.

Lorsch and Allen also compared the performance evaluation systems of their sample of diversified and integrated companies. Their results are consistent with the results of Ackerman and Berg, and the hypotheses of Williamson. The diversified companies rewarded division managers against explicit a priori goals. Rewards were tied directly to the accomplishment of end results. The pool of funds from which rewards were given resulted directly from division profits against the budget. In contrast, division performance evaluation for integrated firms was more informal and was less explicitly related to profit. There was no formula for determining bonus awards, and management exercised more discretion in awarding year end incentive compensation.

The diversified companies placed more emphasis on "end result" criteria, whereas integrated firms used both end result and operating and intermediate measures. The more informal approach and the larger number of measures was possible for the integrated firms, because they pursued less diverse strategies, faced less uncertain environments, and operated more interdependent technologies. Also, there was greater contact between corporate division managers. Alternatively, the diversified companies had more self-contained divisions that facilitated intraorganizational causation analyses, faced more diverse and uncertain tasks, and explicitly measured end result performance. Thus, the study explicitly linked monetary compensation for the diversified companies but not for the integrated ones.

In summary, the research in this area lends itself to interpretation of the linkages between strategy and reward system. Recent research has focused on discussing different reward schemes, and a few studies have related variance in reward systems to variances in strategy and structure. There are fewer direct tests of fit between strategy, reward system, and organization performance, although existing evidence does not reject the linkage.

PEOPLE AND CAREERS

Chandler's original research focused on differences in personality between the strategy formulator and the structure innovator. Nowhere was the contrast greater than between Billy Durant and Alfred P. Sloan at General Motors, but the pattern repeated itself at Du Pont and other organizations which suggested something systematic. Several approaches to considering variations among people are relevant to this issue. First, there is some recent research that attempts to match people with variations in structure and task. Second, there is a great deal of attention now being given to careers and to management development. Finally, practitioners and consulting firms are promoting schemes based on matching individual variations with structure-strategy variations.

A number of studies have attempted to relate variations in personality to variations in task and structure. The first problem encountered with this kind of research is that of establishing valid descriptors to determine personality types. Most of the recent attempts to include personality in contingency theory have used tolerance for ambiguity as the basic dimension of personality that must be matched to task and structure. For the most part, people who are low in tolerance for ambiguity prefer predictable tasks and mechanistic structures (Morse and Young 1973; McCaskey 1976). People who measure high prefer uncertain, changing tasks and organic structures. Another variation uses Jungian types, as measured by the Myers-Briggs indicator (Kilman and Mitroff 1976). The results are quite similar in that these authors also identify personality types that prefer various structural forms, two of which are the organic and mechanistic forms described earlier. Thus, there is some evidence that there are systematic relations between types of people, as measured by tolerance for ambiguity; types of structure, such as mechanistic or organic; and the degree of task uncertainty. Figure 6.3 shows the relation in schematic form. The key is to achieve a fit between the task, the structure, and the people.

Most of the research has not explored the consequences of a lack of fit. Presumably, people are most satisfied and performance is higher when congruence among all the factors is achieved. One study has examined this feature, however (Lorsch and Morse 1974). Again, Lorsch provides the empirical study with ten matched organizations. Four manufacturing firms, two high performers and two low performers, are compared with six research and development laboratories, three high performers and three low performers. The research and development labs performed uncertain tasks, while the manufac-

Figure 6.3 Relations to Include People in Contingency Theory

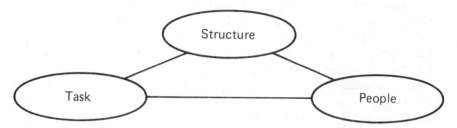

turing plants' task was more predictable.   As predicted, low tolerance for ambiguity was found among the people in the manufacturing plants and high tolerance at the research and development labs. ⌐ The high performing plants had mechanistic structures, the low performing plants had less mechanistic structures.   The high performing research and development labs had organic structures, while the low performers had more formal mechanistic ones. ⌐ Thus, when there was a fit between structure, task, and people, there was higher performance and also greater motivation and satisfaction.   Low performance and motivation occur when the structure is out of line with the task and people. ⌐ Unfortunately, the sample did not contain a situation where personality was out of line with the task.   Therefore, alternative explanations as to causation cannot be rejected.   But, their evidence supports the congruence or fit hypothesis.

The second approach that is relevant for this review is the focus on careers, management development, and career development.   A great deal of current research is focused on these topics (Campbell, Dunette, Lawler, and Weick 1971; Hall 1976; Van Maanen and Schein 1977). However, very little research addresses how variations in strategies and structures are matched with variations in management development practices and career paths.   There is some good work aimed at matching an individual's personal, career, and family development. So far, however, the emphasis of empirical work has been upon the individual; macroperspectives simply have not been taken in empirical studies.   A start in this direction is a study comparing the uses of managerial transfer in European multi-national firms (Edström and Galbraith 1977).   The authors hypothesize that large numbers of transfers of many nationalities lead to a decentralized subsidiary structure.   The work of Pitts is also relevant here (1977).   He finds that firms that grow internally and presumably pursue "related diversification" strategies make use of interdivisional careers to a greater extent than do external growth firms pursuing unrelated diversification strategies.   The need for technology transfer of the "related" competence is satisfied by inter-divisional transfers. Similarly, most organizations that operate a mature matrix organization have career paths that encourage multi-divisional and multi-functional experiences. This form of organization that arises to handle diversity while sharing resources requires generalists who know all the diverse markets, products, countries, and functions. These renaissance people are grown and developed internally by diverse sets of managerial experiences arranged through the career path. The inability to find such people is a primary limitation to the implementation of strategies of extreme diversification. The combination of reward system packages to encourage cooperation and interdivisional careers in matrix and multi-divisional firms has increased the importance of the human resource function. This function is being staffed by talented executives and is being raised in reporting level in the corporation.

The third approach to the people dimension is taken by consulting firms selling strategy making packages to multi-divisional firms. The idea is to match the product division manager with particular stages on the product life cycle, or with whether the product is a "star" or "cow". Entrepreneurial types are needed at maturity. These ideas are very much like Chandler's concepts. However appealing these ideas are, they have yet to be tested. The types of people are also quite vague, being characterized as entrepreneur, sophisticated manager, opportunistic milker, and so on. However, the approach continues to be adopted by companies and by consulting firms.

In summary, there is some evidence that there is something to be gained through systematically matching structure, strategy, and people. At best, such matching gives both human satisfaction and effective organizational performance. Also, there is a great deal that needs to be done in examining which management development and career process best fits different product-market strategies and different structures.

SUMMARY

This chapter begins by reviewing studies that describe actual processes within an organization, distinguishing the actual processes from the more quantitative rational model of the classical theorists. Then, studies showing how these processes vary with strategy and structure are presented and evaluated on the basis of their positive and negative aspects.

Cyert and March introduce the idea that cognitive limits of humans, uncertainty, and lack of agreement over goals produce behavior very different from the view of the classical economist and management scientist. Theorists have corroborated the work of Cyert and March by showing how an investment decision is a long process involving many people and many subdecisions that usually serve to reduce the degree of freedom of the decision making unit. Moreover, theorists have shown how an investment analysis is often tailored to fit the decision of the top manager.

Bower's study distinguished three sequential steps that took place at three different levels in the organization. These steps consisted of the definition of the need for an investment, the impetus where support was obtained, and the approval by corporate management. Ackerman was able to use Bower's model to assign variations in structure. His findings corresponded to previous studies. Integrated firms adopted a more centralized process for allocating capital.

Pointing out the positive and negative aspects associated with structure and process, Williamson says that resources are more likely to be optimally utilized in the multi-divisional firm than they would be in either the functional firm or the holding company, when faced with larger size and diverse businesses. The prime reason he finds is that this structure can provide the information processing system, the control, and the research system necessary for effectiveness.

The research presented on reward systems has focused on different schemes and has related variances in reward systems to variances in strategy and structures. Diversified companies reward division managers on the basis of end results, usually profits. The self-contained division facilitated the explicit measures, and the diversity prevented the informal and more numerous measuring approaches. Integrated firms, however, have a more informal system that is less tied to profitability.

This chapter and the preceeding one have been concerned with the actual processes and systems associated with strategy and structure. In the next chapter, we take a look at additional variables such as the resource allocation process, reward systems, and people and their careers. All of these variables, as we will see, must be designed to fit into a consistent pattern in order for the organization to be most effective.

7

Integration of Dimensions for Strategy Implementation

Our review, thus far, has examined relationships between various dimensions of organization structure and process and the firm's product-market strategy. The intent was to find which structure and process was most appropriate for a particular strategy. With a few exceptions, the relationships examined were between a particular organization dimension, such as the departmental structure or the reward system, and strategy. However, each organizational dimension must be consistent not only with the strategy but also with the others. All the dimensions, such as structure, reward systems, and resource allocation processes, must constitute an internally consistent organizational form. Organizations are packages or mosaics in which all pieces must fit together. This concept of fit, or congruence, was raised earlier in connection with personality types. It will be raised again here, because it is the key concept of current organization design theory and practice.

THE CONCEPT OF FIT

The concept of fit or congruence among all the dimensions of the organization has emerged from several sources. Scott began talking of his stages as consisting "of a cluster of managerial character-istics" (Scott 1971, p. 6). In addition, he suggested that a cluster was not just an organizational form but a "way of managing," even a "way of life". He then identified the characteristics and specified them for each stage. These are shown in Table 7.1.

Table 7.1 Three Stages of Organizational Development

CO. CHARACTERISTICS / STAGE	I	II	III
1. Product line	1. Single product or single line	1. Single product line	1. Multiple product lines
2. Distribution	2. One channel or set of channels	2. One set of channels	2. Multiple channels
3. Organization structure	3. Little or no formal structure—"one man show"	3. Specialization based on function	3. Specialization based on product-market relationships
4. Product-service transactions	4. N/A	4. Integrated pattern of transactions □-□-□ Market	4. Not integrated [A] [B] [C] Markets
5. R & D	5. Not institutionalized-oriented by owner-mgr.	5. Increasingly institutionalized search for product or process improvements	5. Institutionalized search for new products as well as for improvements
6. Performance measurement	6. By personal contact & subjective criteria	6. Increasingly impersonal using technical and/or cost criteria	6. Increasingly impersonal using market criteria (return on investment and market share)
7. Rewards	7. Unsystematic and often paternalistic	7. Increasingly systematic with emphasis on stability and service	7. Increasingly systematic with variability related to performance
8. Control system	8. Personal control of both strategic and operating decisions	8. Personal control of strategic decisions, with increasing delegation of operating decisions based on control by decision rules (policies)	8. Delegation of product-market decisions within existing businesses, with indirect control based on analysis of "results"
9. Strategic choices	9. Needs of owner vs. needs of firm	9. —Degree of integration —Market share objective —Breadth of product line	9. —Entry and exit from industries —Allocation of resources by industry —Rate of growth

This table appears in the case 9–371–294. Copyright © 1971 by the President and Fellows of Harvard College. Reproduced by permission.

The same scheme has been elaborated by consulting firms in their own strategy and structure packages. They distinguished between products or businesses in a multi-divisional firm by the stage of the product life cycle. Then they assume that the "way of managing" will vary with the stages and go on to prescribe managerial characteristics that are appropriate for the various stages. The package currently being used by Hay Associates is shown in Table 7.2. The packages of other firms are similar, with due regard for variations in characteristics and descriptors. The main point is that business

Table 7.2 Hay Associates—Strategic Issues Matrix

			PHASES OF BUSINESS DEVELOPMENT			
			1. EMERGENCE	2. DEVELOPMENTAL	3. MATURE	4. LIQUIDATION
CHARACTERISTICS	A	STYLE CHARACTERISTICS	• Limited Delegation by Strong Leadership • Variety of Schemes Are Possible	•Highest Degree of Delegation and Freedom Supported	•Delegative to Controlled •Flexibility in Meeting Fixed Goals	•Very Limited Delegation and Freedom
	B	DECISION-MAKING CHARACTERISTICS	•Formalized Goals Virtually Nonexistent •Information Limited	•General Goals Exist •More Information for Decisions	•High Degree of Clarity •Information Based Decisions	•Rigid Goals •Information for Control
	C	PLANNING AND CONTROL SYSTEMS CHARACTERISTICS	•Informal, Highly Qualita- tive (Milestone-Oriented)	•Capable of Setting Broad Goals and Measuring Results (Program Oriented)	•Supportive of Careful Goal Setting and Control (P & L Oriented)	•Deemphasize Long-Term Planning, Quantitative. Controls (Balance Sheet Oriented)
	D	RESPONSIVENESS TO EXTERNAL CONDITIONS CHARACTERISTICS	•Limited Responsiveness at First, Focus on Estab- lishing a Position	•Highly Responsive •Adapt to Market Opportu- nities	•Less Responsiveness Required Due to Decreas- ing Rate of Change in Markets	•Responsive But under Very Limited Conditions
	E	INTEGRATION AND DIFFEREN- TIATION CHARACTERISTICS	•High Degree of Differen- tiation among Organization Units •Integration at Top	•Decreasing Differentiation among Units •Integrative Function Be- coming More "Local" to Markets, Products	•Continuing Decrease in Differentiation •Integration "Local"	•Low Differentiation •Integration at the Top (Corporate)
	F	LEADERSHIP CHARACTERISTICS	•Entrepreneur, Strong Leader	•Entrepreneur/Business Manager	•Sophisticated Manager	•Administrator, S.O.B.
	G	MOTIVATIONS CHARACTERISTICS	•Venturesome •Accepts Unaccustomed Risks	•Venturesome to Conser- vative •Accustomed and Unaccus- tomed Risks	•Conservative Primarily •Generally Risk-Adverse	•Conservative •Risk Adverse
	H	REWARD MANAGEMENT CHARACTERISTICS	•High Base Compensation to Attract People •Discretionary Bonus	•High Levels Related to Job •Incentives for Building Results	•More Average Levels Related to Job •Incentives for Results Above High Goal	•Average Level •Incentives for Cost Control
	I	KNOW-HOW AND DEVELOPMENT CHARACTERISTICS	•Know-How Depth Impor- tant Near Top •Development Needed to Support Expected Expansion	•Ever Broadening Scope and Increasing Numbers of Managers Required	•Development Needs and Know-How Becoming Specialized, Static	•Specialized Depth and Scope of Know-How

Reprinted by special permission of Hay Associates.

divisions need to adopt an internally consistent set of practices in order to implement the product strategy effectively.

Another source of development of the congruence or fit concept is organization theory. Leavitt was one of the first to discuss the degree to which task, structure, people, and processes form an integrated whole (Leavitt 1960, 1965). He suggests that organizational change strategies should take all dimensions into account. One cannot successfully change structure without making compensating and reinforcing changes in information and budgeting systems, career systems, management development practices, and compensation policies. In organizations, everything is connected to everything else.

The major developer and empirical investigator of the fit concept has been Jay Lorsch (Lawrence and Lorsch 1967; Lorsch and Allen 1973; Lorsch and Morse 1974). Much of his work has already been discussed in the sections devoted to the individual dimensions. He is the primary investigator to examine structure, task, people and administrative practices; the congruence between these dimensions; and the degree to which congruence is related to organizational performance. The results of his research support the hypothesis that a fit between the dimensions leads to high organizational performance. Those organizations that were not high performers were experiencing a situation in which either structure or process did not fit with the degree of task uncertainty.

Two other studies also support the concept of fit or congruence. Using the same data base mentioned before, Khandwalla proposed that internal consistency of structural design was related to performance (Khandwalla, 1973). He found that it was the more effective firms that adopted uncertainty reducers, internally differentiated their structures, formalized procedures, and decentralized decisions all in proportion to one another. There was far less congruence between these practices in less effective firms. These findings led him to suggest that it was the whole package or *gestalt* that was more important than any single factor acting alone.

Some preliminary results of a study by Child also reinforce this hypothesis. He is studying five international airlines, their structures and their performance. In examining the two most profitable airlines, he finds that they have contrasting administrative practices and structures even though they face similar problems, have similar route structures, and equivalent sizes. But the one feature they have in common is congruence among their processes and structure. One is not divisionalized, has short time horizons, is centralized, and uses high and continuous involvement of the top management team which meets often. It operates a personal control process and has open communications among a management cadre which has long tenure. Conflicts are expressed and decisions are made and acted upon rapidly. The other airline has a multi-divisional, regional form with decentralized profit centers. It operates with impersonal controls and sophisticated planning processes. It has a large number of administrative staff personnel who operate the impersonal control system. These observations lead Child to suggest that it is the consistency among these practices, structure and people that makes them effective.

The poor performers also had multi-divisional structures for decentralization but placed restrictions on the amount of discretion that could be exercised. Although they had the structure and incurred the administrative cost of large staff overhead, they received none of the benefits of decentralization. Child's explanation of the effect of inconsistency upon performance is based on its impact on managerial behavior. The inconsistent practices give mixed signals that frustrate managers and weaken their motivation.

Thus, there are three researchers that have offered data to support the consistency or congruence hypothesis. These studies should be followed by others using different methodologies, however, because the above research is methodology bound. That is, each of the studies is a small sample, cross sectional, comparative study. This methodology could lead to rejection of the fit hypothesis and has not. But it has several flaws. The concept of fit involves consistency among multiple organizational dimensions, performance, and strategy. Consequently, a small sample size does not permit a fully orthogonal experimental design. Thus, there are still multiple interpretations that cannot be rejected either. Some of these interpretations concern causation. For example, does noninvolvement of corporate offices create the autonomy that divisions use to respond to the uniqueness of their market, thereby performing at a high level? Or, does high divisional performance create confidence in the minds of corporate management, who then give high performing divisions autonomy while concentrating on the low performing divisions? Here the cross-sectional nature of the research does not permit a rejection of the alternative explanations. Some large sample and longitudinal empirical studies are needed to complement and build upon the Lorsch, Khandwalla, and Child research.

Some further conceptual development has recently appeared (Galbraith 1977). Galbraith has built upon both the Lorsch scheme and the Lorsch research. He has attempted to identify the major design variables to be considered when matching organization form to strategy. These are shown schematically in Figure 7.1.

The product-market strategy chosen by the firm determines to a large extent the task diversity and uncertainty with which the organization must cope. The organization must then match the people with task through selection, recruitment, and training and development practices. The people must also match the structure. The structure, also chosen to fit the task, is specified by choices of the division of labor (amount of role differentiation), the departmental structure, the shape (number of levels, spans of control), and the distributions of power (both horizontal and vertical). Across the structure, processes are overlaid to allocate resources and co-ordinate activities not handled by the departmental structure. These information and decision processes are planning and control systems, budgeting processes, integration mechanisms, and performance measurements. And finally, the reward system must be matched with the task and structure through choices of compensation practices, career paths, leader behavior, and the design of work. In total, all these choices must create an internally consistent design. If one of the practices is changed, the other dimensions must be altered to maintain fit. Similarly, if the strategy is changed, then all the dimensions may need to be altered so that the form of organization remains consistent with the product-market strategy.

There is a great deal of research yet to be done in testing the concept of congruence, because it comprises many interacting variables. Although the concept of fit is a useful one, it lacks the precise definition needed to test it and to recognize whether an organization has it or not. There is also a trade-off between short-run fit and long-run fit. That is, the short-run congruence between all the organization design variables may be so good that they cannot be disentangled and rearranged into a new configuration in order to meet an environmental challenge or to implement a new strategy. For example, the Swiss watch makers achieved an excellent fit between strategy and structure for the making of mechanical watches. The institutionalization of the mechanical technology has prevented these firms from adapting to the new technology. The fit is so strong that the Swiss became ready buyers from American watch makers who wanted to dump their subsidiaries (Miles and Cameron 1977). Thus the corporate designer must choose a time over which to optimize the fit.

In the next section we want to describe an organization that has achieved fit for a period of time.

Figure 7.1 Major Illustration of Fit Among an Organization's Design Variables

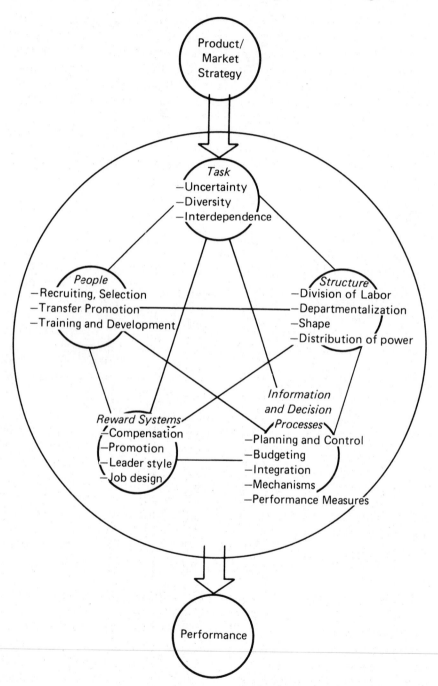

AN EXAMPLE: DOW–CORNING

Dow-Corning has been much publicized as an organization that adopted a top level matrix structure in the middle 1960s (Goggins 1974). At this time, it has fine tuned its structure, added additional supporting systems, and blended them into its worldwide matrix structure. Before describing the current organization form, we will give a brief description of its history and prior structure. Dow-Corning is a joint venture created by Dow Chemical (50 percent) and Corning Glass (50 percent) around 1942 in order to pursue silicon based products. From its creation until 1962, Dow-Corning was managed in an entrepreneurial start up mode. The growing organization was managed through a centralized, functional structure that placed emphasis on technology and product development. Dow-Corning was to pursue a product diversification strategy, but the products were related by all drawing upon silicon technology.

This organization grew into a $50 million business, employing 1,500 people by 1962. At that time, there was a sharp change in management. The growth, the product diversity, and the new product development process could not be managed out of a single profit center. A new chief executive was brought in from Corning Glass to introduce a multi-divisional structure consisting of five product profit centers and functional staffs with dotted line reporting relations to the functional departments within the divisions. This change achieved integration across the functions around product application, turned around the profit situation, and continued growth.

The multi-divisional structure began experiencing several problems. The expansion into international markets caused competition between domestic and foreign investments and produced another source of diversity with which to cope. Manufacturing could not be broken apart by product, as one plant made materials for all divisions. The transfer price-investment controversy naturally arose. Much technology was applicable to all divisions but not shared during the competition. The central research and development unit atrophied from neglect. Then, when a minirecession hit the industry and profits fell 35 percent, a new chief executive was brought in from Dow.

In 1967, Goggins became president and began to implement the matrix on the domestic side of the organization. The five divisions were converted to ten business profit centers. The functional departments reported to both the business manager and their functional vice-president. This structure is shown in Figure 7.2. This move increased the influence of the functions and created the balance of power that characterizes the matrix. The wide span of control is managed by an office of the chief executive consisting of the president and board chairman. An attempt was made to organize within the function by product as much as possible. The subfunction managers from each function sit on the business board, which is the policy making body for that business.

Figure 7.2 The Dow-Corning Matrix

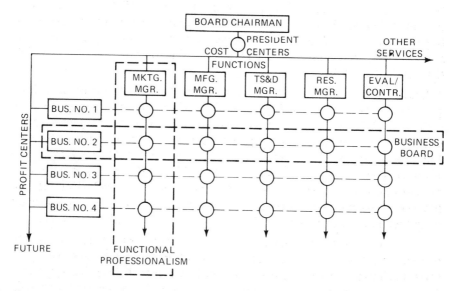

In addition to the hierarchy and the ten business boards, a number of other systems and processes are used in order to enable the firm to continue to grow and to develop new products, (30 percent of sales come from products introduced in the last five years). The products that move across the functions are assigned to business areas having a product manager and a product board. The product manager is usually a subfunction manager who wears two hats. The board consists of representatives from the other functions. The leadership of the product boards changes with phases in the product life. Early phases are dominated by research and product development, then by manufacturing, and so on.

The dual reporting relations, two-hat product managers, and substantial new product activity all generate a good deal of cross product and cross functional conflict. In order to see that the conflict is constructive and constructively resolved, it is channeled into the planning process. Dow-Corning has the standard rolling five year long-range plan where year one drops out as the budget. In controlling against this plan, the top group meets weekly to hear each business and function in turn. Interunit conflicts are raised and resolved. Twice a year all business groups, functional departments, and regional managers come together for three days to formulate and update the strategies and plans. The conflict is channeled into a process that leads to its resolution. The matrix generates conflict from its multiple dimensions. It is channeled into a planning process where a tie breaker exists if agreement does not naturally result. All successful matrix organizations have an effective planning process into which the conflict is channeled.

2. There is also a strong emphasis on goal setting and on an MBO program. Again, the ability to work against agreed upon goals permits a well functioning matrix. Because people work against goals and problems, rather than against each other, they have less need for hierarchy and tie breaking. For more on MBO programs, see Richard's book in this series (1978). The MBO program requires multi-dimensional profit and cost reporting. As each side of the matrix needs its own information and evaluation system, a great deal of effort goes into these multi-dimensional information systems.

The MBO program serves as an input into the performance appraisal process. Each manager is evaluated against objectives. The subfunctional managers receive a joint evaluation from business and functional managers. Here again, the agreed upon objectives help in reaching consensus. As in most organizations, if there is substantial disagreement, the functional manager has the final say. The managers at the top also receive incentive compensation based on *total* company profit. Business and area managers have their own profit center, but they receive a bonus for total company profit in order to increase the likelihood of cooperation and effective handling of conflict. Bonuses are paid against planned profit.

The business and product boards are able to function well for other reasons. Most people selected to participate on boards have a common technical background. Almost all managers are chemical engineers. In addition, the career path is multi-functional, providing experience on both business and functional sides. This career system gives board members a sound understanding of other persons' problems and facilitates general all-around communication, so that people are less concerned about territory or turf. Finally, all product and business board participants are sent to Phase I of the Blake Grid prior to taking a board assignment (Blake and Mouton

1964). This training in group problem solving and conflict, followed immediately by experiences utilizing the training, reinforces the ability of this organization to handle matrix conflict constructively. Thus the selection process, the career path, and the management development practices create the people needed to make the matrix work.

The integration mechanisms are further reinforced by the physical setting, which is specifically designed for their organization. All boards are colocated in open offices, with business meeting rooms displaying business information. This gives a sense of common territory and facilitates informal day-to-day communication across functions.

In summary, Dow-Corning has adopted an organization form that fits its strategy, technology, and current size. It is pursuing a strategy of product diversification, although each product and business is related to silicon technology. New product introduction is the key competitive issue, which requires sophisticated technology, manufacturing economies of scale, and tight integration across functions. When combined with the moderate size of the business, these factors require a balance between functions and products—that is, a matrix. In order to work a matrix, the organization must handle conflict and cooperation across all units. The planning process, with its frequent meetings, its multi-dimensional profit and cost reporting, and its MBO program, plays a significant role in conflict management. It is backed up with companywide incentive compensation, business and product boards, multi-function and multi-business careers, conflict management training, and colocation of boards. Together these structures, systems, and processes make a successful package that works for Dow-Corning at this stage in its development.

The purpose of the example is not to sell the matrix organization, which is not solely responsible for Dow-Corning's performance. The purpose is to discuss the fit among all the dimensions of the organization. It is the authors' belief that the fit, along with the technology, financial policies, and so on, is partially responsible for the successful performance. If circumstances such as technology change, Dow-Corning should abandon the matrix. However, Dow-Corning must then achieve another fit between all its systems and processes in order to fit its new strategy. It is this total change that makes the transition from one stage to another so difficult. It is also this total change and the difficulty in changing that has led Chandler and others to talk of stages of development and a stagewise development model. We will review these in the next chapter.

SUMMARY

This chapter examined the concept of fit or congruence among all dimensions of the organization.

Scott, as well as various consulting firms, has identified stages of growth and has shown how each stage is associated with a cluster of managerial characteristics which constitute a "way of life" during that stage. Identification of the characteristics and stages is of utmost importance, because businesses need to adopt an internally consistent set of practices in order to implement their product strategy effectively.

Leavitt was one of the first to discuss the degree to which task, structure, people, and process form an integrated whole. He suggests that organizational change strategies should take all the dimensions into account. Lorsch, who has been the major empirical tester of the concept of fit, has made an explicit attempt to relate practices and fit to organizational performance. He found that the organizations that were high performers were the ones that experienced a fit. However, the research is methodologically bound, and more needs to be done in this area.

Galbraith has built on Lorsch's research and Leavitt's ideas in an attempt to identify major design variables to be considered when matching organization form to strategy. His schema depicts how the firm's product-market strategy determines the task diversity and uncertainty with which an organization must cope. The organization must also match the people with the task through selection, recruitment, training, and development. The structure, information and decision processes, and reward systems must also fit to form the integrated whole.

The chapter concludes with an example of how Dow-Corning has achieved this fit. Since fit is a difficult state to achieve, movements between successive states of fit have been proposed to be stages of corporate development. The next chapter focuses on this stagewise development.

8

Growth and
Development Models

This chapter will review and compare the stages of growth models and empirical studies by various authors. The preceding chapters presented material relevant to the question of whether strategy and structure were related. The conclusion was that, with some qualification, they were related. Also, it was argued that the various structures consisted of many dimensions in addition to departmental structure, and the important design problem was to achieve a fit between all the dimensions. Thus, restructuring is a major undertaking that moves an organization to a qualitatively different form. When a number of organizations repeat the same sequence of major structural changes, researchers propose that something systematic is at work and that there may be different stages of organizational growth involved, with each stage having its own peculiar combination of structure, process, reward and people dimensions. In this chapter, we will review the various models that have been proposed for different strategy-structure stages of growth and development.

Every area of inquiry has its own stages model. One can find proposed stages in individual cognitive development and socioemotional development, in group development, and in the economic development of countries. Organization and management theory is no exception. Several reviews of this literature already exist and will not be repeated here (Starbuck 1965, 1971; Child and Keiser 1978). Instead, we will select only those models that are relevant to choices of strategy and structure. These models are referred to as metamorphosis models, as opposed to continuous, smooth development models.

METAMORPHOSIS MODELS

Metamorphosis models of development are based on the premise that growth is not smooth and continuous, but is characterized instead by abrupt, discrete, and substantial changes in organizational strategy and structure. That is, organization structures are systems of limited adaptability. The structural parameters of the organization are capable of providing adjustments to routine disturbances such as daily operating problems and the turnover of non-central personnel. But long-run shifts such as technological change, change of government, and the like pose problems for which the existing set of structural parameters cannot adequately provide smooth adaptation. In order to return the organization to equilibrium with its environment, a metamorphosis is required. That is, a simple alteration in structure or rewards will be inadequate. The entire constellation of systems, rewards, processes, and structures must be disengaged, realigned, and then reconnected. For these reasons strategy and structure changes are major undertakings, and a complete transition often requires up to five years. It is usually hypothesized that a crisis is necessary to provoke the effort to change the status quo power structure (Greiner 1972).

A number of metamorphosis growth models have been offered. They vary in the number of stages that constitute the developmental sequence, in the number of organizational strategy and structure dimensions that are included, and in the particular determinant that drives the metamorphosis, for example, age, size or complexity. The latter distinction accounts for the greatest variance in the models. For example, James (1974) has proposed a growth model based on time phases or age of the organization, whereas Pugh and his colleagues (1969) propose that size is the primary driving force generating changes in organization form. The problem with all of these models is not that they are wrong, but that they are only partially correct. Clearly, young organizations are different from old ones. They have fewer institutionalized practices and are more entrepreneurial, creative, informal, and fragile. Similarly, a fifty person organization is very different from one that has fifty thousand, and there are major transitions along the way to the latter size. In reality age, size, and complexity are confounded, and it is virtually impossible to disentangle their separate effects. All contribute to development. Which model one uses will vary to some extent with the questions that one is asking. Because we are interested in choices of strategy and structure, the complexity models are most relevant for our purposes.

In the next sections we will review the most relevant complexity models that have followed from Chandler's work, giving particular attention to the empirical studies that have also followed. We want to focus upon the following questions: What constitutes a stage in these developmental sequences? How many are there? Is the sequence unalterable? And how do you know one stage from another?

COMPLEXITY GROWTH STAGES

The stages of growth models of interest here also grew out of the Chandler research. His work has been summarized and extended by Scott (1971), whose model was presented earlier in the chapter on contingency relations. His three stage model will be the primary focus in this chapter.

SCOTT'S THREE STAGE MODEL

The Scott three stage model, however, does not include all of Chandler's stages. Recall that Chandler proposed a sequence of changes that begins with the small enterprise. He suggested that the first strategy was simply an expansion of volume. The increase in output required separation of an administrative component, that is distinct from the work performing component. The next strategy was to increase volume by expanding geographically. The multiple geographic units posed new administrative problems with regard to headquarters—field unit relations. This problem is the classic centralization-decentralization issue. These two forms are grouped together to form stage I in the Scott model. The result is a simple organization performing a single function, such as manufacturing, for a single product line. It provides a good starting point for the complexity models.

The first increase in complexity by American firms was initiated by a strategy of vertical integration. That is, the simple firm began to acquire other functions, such as the distribution and selling functions. By this means, diverse functions were added. These sequential functions posed new administrative problems in managing horizontal work flows, however. The result was the invention of the functional organization and of processes of forecasting and scheduling. These firms learned to manage multiple functions, but remained within a single product line. This type of firm was Scott's stage II form.

The next stage starts with the pursuit of a strategy of product diversification. The management of multiple product lines posed problems of measurement of relative financial performance and allocation of capital across product lines. These problems were resolved by the adoption of the multi-divisional structure in which each division was a functional organization producing a single product or limited line of products. Each division operated as a profit center. This profit divisionalized firm was Scott's stage III model. Table 7.1 summarizes Scott's elaboration of Chandler's work based on the research that has taken place since 1960. Scott extends the changes in structure to include changes in rewards, control, and so on. This model has been the most popular and widely quoted of the development models.

The essence of the Chandler and Scott sequences is the successive addition of new sources of diversity which result in more complexity. Starting with the simple firm which is single product, single function, and single region, there are successive adoptions of multiple regions, then multiple functions, and finally multiple products as the firm becomes a stage I, stage II and finally stage III organization. The change from stage to stage constitutes a metamorphosis.

SALTER MODEL

The Scott model has been analyzed and extended by Salter (1970). He suggested that the Scott model misses two forms of organization and thereby also misses the possible alternative paths that can be taken through developmental sequences. For example, the multi-divisional forms that were adopted by General Motors and Du Pont were achieved through different transitions. General Motors was a holding company, while Du Pont was a stage II functional organization. The holding company form is not in the model. In addition Salter proposes that the geographic multidivisional form should be a separate stage. Thus he splits Scott's stage III form into a stage 3, the geographic form, and a stage 4, the product form. However, he does not include the holding company as a separate form or stage.

The Salter work raises the question of what constitutes a stage. A multi-divisional structure around geographic areas is different from a multi-divisional structure around product lines. But is it different enough to constitute a separate stage? How different must it be? How does one tell? Our view is that the geographic profit center is not a separate stage. Although the transition from geographic to product divisionalized form or vice versa would require a major change in the power structure of an organization, it would not constitute a major change in the "way of life" in the organization. It is still a profit center or investment center of one dimension (i. e., product or region). The managerial style is still one of delegation of operations to the divisions, and the rewards are based on bottom line results. There is nowhere near the magnitude of change that occurs in the change from a functional form to a profit center form. It is our contention that characteristics of structure, process, reward, and people are quite similar for all multi-divisional forms regardless of what the one dimension is. That is, the multi-divisional structure can be based upon products, regions, markets, industries and so on, and the "way of life" will be similar. That way of life will change only when other dimensions or sources of diversity are added, or when the geographic expansion is international rather than domestic.

STOPFORD'S MODEL

Another extension of the Scott model has been proposed by Stopford to account for the international expansion of American firms (Stopford 1968; Stopford and Wells 1973). Recall from our review of his work in Chapter 3 that he identified a two stage model into international markets. First, the firms formed an international division and attached it to their domestic product divisions. Then the division was disbanded, and either worldwide product divisions or area divisions were adopted. Product divisions resulted from high foreign product diversification, and area divisions were adopted for low product diversity. However, Stopford did not suggest that these structural forms constituted a new stage. Instead he called them stage III with an international division and stage III other, meaning that the form could be product, area, or even some mixture of the two. The question naturally arises whether these two types are in fact stage IV and V, in fact a type genuinely different from stage III domestic firms.

Our view is that the international division is not a new stage. The addition of a new geographic division, even an international division, has about the same impact as the addition of a new business or product division. The move to a global structure of either worldwide product divisions or area divisions poses a problem, however. On the one hand, the global structures are still uni-dimensional profit centers. On the other hand, the global structures are significant departures from the pure domestic multi-divisional structure. In addition there is no single global form. An organization can be a global-divisional structure as already mentioned, a global holding company, or a global functional organization. We will deal first with how the global structures differ from pure domestic forms then with differences among the multiple forms.

The difference between global and domestic multi-divisionals is best illustrated by the phases through which the global structure is established. It takes place over an extended period of time and entails establishing an international operation which is integrated with domestic operations. Both operations are modified in the process of becoming a global company. The transition is best illustrated by the work of Smith and Charmoz (1975) in their analysis of American pharmaceutical companies which expanded internationally. Since their work was not presented earlier, it will be reviewed briefly here.

SMITH AND CHARMOZ MODEL

Smith and Charmoz report that predictable problems arise in the growth of the multi-national corporations, because the U.S. organization must invent coordination and control devices in the international sphere, since the existing devices were designed for domestic operations. They invented control mechanisms for domestic operations before going international; therefore they must start again with Stages I, II, III on an international basis. The evolution is one of establishing control points that move from country to the corporate level, as the organization moves from the initial steps to a global enterprise. They propose a five phase model for this evolution which is illustrated in Figure 8.1.

Phase I represents the first move into a new area, an action that is guided by an attempt to minimize risk. The capital risk is minimized by using local distributors and participating in joint ventures. This allows the U.S. firm to "learn the ropes." Often, returns on the original investments are held as reserves against future losses. During this phase, there are no systems to process international information, no international staffs, and no plans or strategies. Decisions are made through direct personal contract as problems arise. Control is located at the corporate office, because new operations need cash.

An overload at the top provokes a move to Phase II. Either too many decisions must be made, or not enough decisions are made.

Figure 8.1 Evolution of Control, Coordination, and Organizational Crises in the Development of MNC

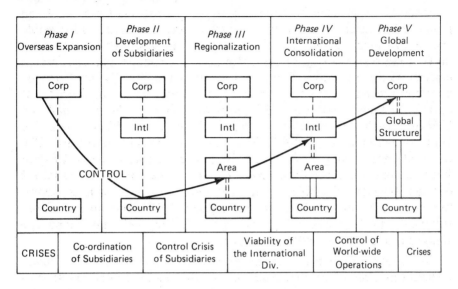

Coordination Patterns

— — —   Mutual Adjustment (Coordination by checking only as problems arise)

= = = =   Planning (Coordination through tops down planning)

════════   Policy and Procedure (Coordination through   establishment of policies and procedures)

SOURCE: Smith and Charmoz 1975.

Whatever the case may be, the result is that the subsidiaries go their own way. Also, because of lack of time and expertise at the top, poor decisions often are made.

Phase II is marked by subsidiary development and the appointment of an international executive and staff. The executive acts to support the subsidiaries and allocates capital accordingly. Large subsidiaries therefore get the most attention, because they require most of the investment. Control now moves into the hands of the subsidiaries, who initiate, propose, and act. The domestic company is essentially left out of the process because of its lack of knowledge. Up to this point, there has been little movement of people to the international division, and U.S. centered thinking still predominates. Control remains on a basis of personal contact between the international executive and both corporate offices and the subsidiaries. By the end of Phase II, however, the international executive becomes overwhelmed. He is continuously traveling and has little, if any, time left to plan. Subsidiary managers begin to run their subsidiaries according to their own needs, not the corporate office's. Competition between subsidiaries develops over new areas and territories.

Phase III, then, can be called the phase of regionalization. A regional international executive is added, as well as staffs, and possible rationalizations are made for cross-border moves. These moves require a regional plan. Impersonal planning control replaces personal contact as control moves from subsidiary to region. By now the corporation recognizes the international group as a source of investment and is no longer satisfied with informal personal decision making. Use of return on investment criteria is instituted either across the board or is modified for the differential risk levels of countries. The international president is now a politician, a buffer. Since little data is available for making decisions, the domestic executives are ignorant of the international affairs. The international president must simultaneously get support from domestic product divisions and ward off ignorant staff groups who want information and may flood the fledgling subsidiaries with procedures.

The international president may be seen as a block by both international and domestic subsidiaries. At this point, the domestic subsidiaries and corporate offices realize how little they know about the international group and notice that the international group is a competitor for capital, research and development, people, and so forth. The problem at this point, however, is to prevent a move to a global structure that would be premature, because staffs are still ignorant about international affairs, and there are no planning and information systems to provide a link with the corporate office.

Phase IV is marked by international consolidation. In this stage, control moves to the international CEO to bring order and rationality to the dispersion characterizing the previous three periods of development. This period is one in which the corporate officers take a real and direct interest in the international divisions. The size of investments and interdependency of areas dictate a greater degree of centralization. However, there are no blanket solutions here, because of the differential rate of development of the geographic areas and the firm's own product lines. It is in the establishment of distinctive patterns of coordination that most firms differ. International consolidation is marked by executive international committees, planning and evaluation systems, more sophisticated financial measures, and task forces. By now the international division rivals the domestic divisions even more. There is an increasingly greater need for worldwide data and for a global mechanism to overcome parochial local interests. The corporate staff wants more control and information at this point; the area managers resent the planning and control. The international executive may again moderate a still ignorant staff, since the corporate officers might press prematurely for the kind of "planning control" that is better suited for the next phase of development.

Phase V, which can be termed "global development," is marked by corporate control. Through the increased contacts of the previous phase, corporate and domestic product groups have a more realistic awareness of foreign operations. The "planning" coordination provided by the international division is now superfluous. The particular organizational format that evolves is governed by product diversity and proportion of foreign sales as presented by Stopford. Phase V is also marked by significant improvements in global information and planning systems. Most companies maintain some form of international specialist coordination. This role is more integrative than controlling.

Our view is that transition to a global structure constitutes a metamorphosis. There are changes in the financial control system designed to handle such factors as national variations, profits by product and region, and transfer pricing. Different and multiple standards of evaluation appear; careers and compensation practices are changed; new committees and staffs evolve. Most important, an international mentality gets created to various degrees. All together, we feel these changes constitute a different "way of life" and therefore a different form.

The global form is not, however, a single distinct form like a functional or holding company form. There is no single global form. In its different manifestations it resembles the multi-divisional forms which are all profit centers, but in which the profit center could be based on products, markets, or regions. Global structures can also assume any of those three multi-divisional forms, or they can take global functional or a holding company form. In fact Franko's description of European mother-daughter forms are descriptions of global holding companies. Thus we conceive of four different types of organization, each of which constitutes a distinct way of life—the simple, the functional, the holding company (or conglomerate), and the multi-divisional form. Each of these, but probably only the latter three, can exist in a domestic or in a global form. We prefer to talk about these eight possible organizations as forms rather than stages. All the forms are possible. Whether there are stages is in part an empirical question. Two studies have addressed themselves to this question.

STOPFORD AND FRANKO STUDIES

Two major empirical studies by Stopford and Wells (1972) and Franko (1974, 1977) have dealt with the stage of growth of American multi-nationals and European multi-nationals, respectively. These studies have both been discussed earlier in this paper. It is important at this point, however, to focus on their findings concerning the sequence of the stages. Figure 8.2 illustrates, comparatively, the sequence of both American and European multi-nationals (Franko 1977).

The American multi-national's first phase in international growth is characterized by an initial period of autonomy for the foreign subsidiary. The second phase is a period of organizational consolidation when an international division is developed. The international division is typically considered an independent enterprise and is not subject to the same strategic planning that guides domestic activities. In the third phase, strategic planning is carried out on a consistent and worldwide basis, and the structure of the foreign activities is altered to provide closer links with the rest of the structure. As indicated by the chart, most American firms went through one of two major sequences of structural change. Either they moved from a functional Stage II structure to a divisional Stage III structure for their domestic businesses before adding an international division, or they added an international division to a domestic Stage III structure. The figure also indicates that forty-nine of fifty-seven firms that replaced their international divisions did so after they had developed Stage III structures for their domestic activities. The few firms that moved directly from a Stage II structure with an international division to a global system are exceptions to the trend, and all of them adopted area divisions.

> Only twenty-four firms, or *14 percent of the 170 firms*, have moved directly from the phase of autonomous subsidiaries to a global structure without ever using an international division. In almost every instance, these firms have expanded abroad primarily by acquisitions or mergers with other firms that had international interests.
>
> Only six cases of firms reversing the directions of change were observed. These reversals are associated with failures in the decentralized systems and with decisions to recentralize authority and to establish tighter controls. (Stopford and Wells 1972, p. 48).

Unlike American multi-nationals, the continental enterprises that adopted supranational organization structures typically did so after

Figure 8.2 International Organizational Evolution of Multinational Enterprise

Continental Multinational Enterprise

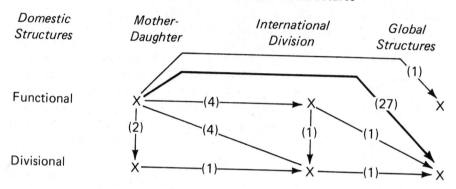

American Multinational Enterprise

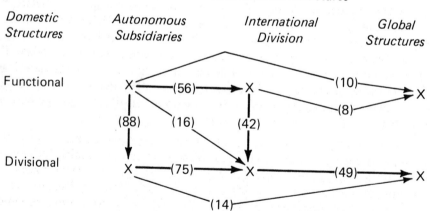

SOURCES: For Continental Multi-national Enterprise: CEI-Harvard Comparative Multi-national Enterprise Project. For U.S. Enterprise, Stopford and Wells 1972, p. 28.

achieving a relatively large spread of multi-national operations. Moreover, when the continental multi-nationals changed their organization structures, they also did so in a sequence very different from that followed by their American counterparts.

One sees that most continental firms simply skipped the international division phase passed through by nearly 90 percent of the 170 American multi-nationals surveyed by the Comparative Multi-national Enterprise Project. One also observes that in all but three cases, Continental moves to the global forms of worldwide product divisions, area divisions, or mixed and matrix structures accompanied rather than followed divisionalization moves at home. In contrast, more than three-quarters of the American enterprises classified as multi-national saw fit to change their domestic organization structures from functional to divisional prior to adopting one of the so-called global structures.

In the competitive environment of their home market, American firms adapted their structures to their product diversification strategies. In practice, this meant that diversified American firms forsook functional for divisional organization structures well before they had had much of a chance to involve themselves in foreign operations.

Further examination of the data reveals some consistency between the European and American experiences. Those firms that did establish international divisions were French and German firms which came from large countries with large domestic markets. Also, if Europe is considered a single market, then many firms manage the rest of the world through an international division. Both these observations lend support to the international division stage, provided that there is a large domestic market.

In summary, these studies support the stagewise thesis of growth from a domestic functional organization to global multi-divisional structures. They also repeat Salter's assertion of alternate paths to worldwide structures. As organizations come from different sized countries, face domestic markets varying in competitiveness, and grow by acquisition rather than internally, they choose different but predictable paths to a similar final stage. However, the more detailed the specification of the stage, the less predictable the sequential movement. As long as we conceive of only three stages, with global forms considered to be a Stage III type, the stages of growth model holds. As soon as we consider other types of global structure or consider substages such as the international division phase, more alternate paths appear, more outcomes are possible, and more detailed specifications of strategy, such as Rumelt's nine categories, are required in order to match strategy with structure and process.

A REVISED MODEL

In this section we would like to offer our model of growth and development which summarizes the thinking of others and builds on the empirical evidence. The model is based upon several assumptions and
empirical findings. First it is assumed that, starting with the simple
form, any source of diversity could be added to move to a new form.
There is no set sequence through which firms must move in lock step.
An organization could add functions, products, and geography and
wind up with a global multi-divisional structure passing through functional and domestic multi-divisional forms along the way. Or it could
add functions, geography, and products and still wind up with a global
multi-divisional form by passing instead through functional and global
functional forms as intermediate transitions. As a result of this assumption, alternate paths through the developmental sequence are possible. The comparison of American and European multi-nationals is
a case in point.

Although there are possible alternative paths, a dominant sequence
emerges empirically. Both Franko and Stopford report dominant sequences when multiple sequences are possible. This result is attributable in part to the effects of the environment. When faced with
similar environments, firms choose to do similar things. The particular scenario that emerged consisted of specific patterns of population
growth, economic growth, technological change, political changes, and
world wars. Particular strategies resulting in particular structures
proved to be profitable at various times. However, if a different
scenario could have emerged, then a different dominant sequence
would be observed. The point is that there is no set sequence; in all
cases, however, development was dominated by the particular pattern
of organization growth. Even though a pattern dominates, there are
other routes taken by a minority of the firms.

Another feature of all developmental models is that an organization
can stop anywhere along the way. Not every American organization
is going to become a global, multi-divisional form. Various niches can
be found, and any of the forms can be adopted which happen to fit that
niche. Also, a firm can reverse direction and retrace its steps. Some
firms are busy selling off their international subsidiaries and could
very well move back to a domestic multi-divisional.

Finally, the resulting structure of any sequence of development is,
as Chandler suggested, a concatenation of all previous steps. If one
examined global structure based on areas, one would find that, within
an area, structure is based on products. Within the product substruc-

ture, the organization could be market based by breaking out government and commercial sectors. Within a market sector, the substructure is probably functional. Thus each level of the hierarchy is a mechanism for coping with a source of diversity.

The resulting stages model is shown in Figure 8.3. The starting point is the simple structure with one function and product line. The

Figure 8.3 A Summary of Stages Model

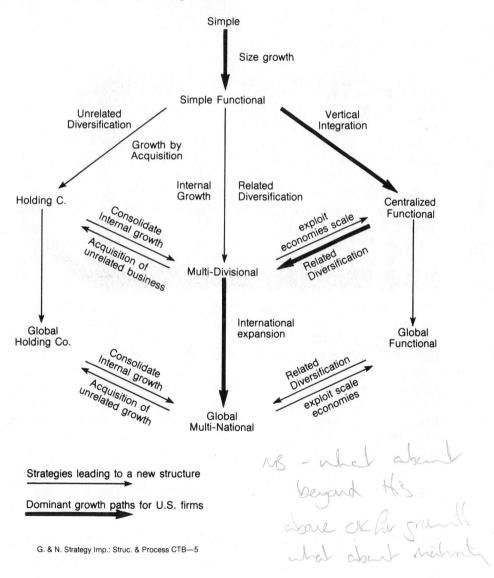

first major structural change results from a growth in volume. The increased size brings about a division of labor and the simple functional organization to coordinate the divided work. From this structure several paths are possible. Some firms with crucial supply or distribution problems will pursue strategies of vertical integration. These forms will continue to elaborate the functional organization into large, centralized firms. The mining companies are good examples. Other organizations will diversify product lines through internal growth and acquisition. The internal developer tending to pursue a related diversification strategy will adopt the multi-divisional structure. The third path an organization can follow is to diversify through acquisition and pursue an unrelated diversification strategy. These firms would adopt a holding company or conglomerate form. In each case the structure fits the strategy.

Although the next stages increase rapidly in number of possibilities, empirically there is a dominant movement. The majority of large enterprises have moved to the multi-divisional form either from a holding company type like General Motors, or from a functional form as did Du Pont. In the former case the move is an attempt to consolidate acquisitions, exploit a source of relatedness, and switch to internal growth. The latter case is the classic example of a functional organization unable to manage diversity.

Two other possible paths are not observed in the particular sample of firms that make up the empirical study. The multi-divisional could change to the centralized functional form or to the holding company model. A firm could introduce standardization across related product lines and attempt to exploit economies of scale by moving to the functional organization. General Motors may be an example. In its automobile business General Motors moved towards a functional organization by placing all manufacturing in a GM Assembly Division. Alternatively, the multi-divisional firm could pursue external growth and diversify into less related businesses. A transition to a holding company could occur if the new acquisitions are not integrated into the existing structure. The original core business will probably become an autonomous group managed from a small headquarters office that has been removed from its original location. There probably are examples of organizations not on the *Fortune 500* that have followed these paths.

The next different stage of development for those organizations that choose to pursue strategies of international expansion is the global form. Most organizations will adopt either the area or product global form as indicated in the Stopford research. Global holding companies and global functional forms are possible too, although less likely.

In summary, firms do follow developmental sequences characterized by a metamorphosis between the stages. There is also a dominant path that has been followed by large American enterprises. However, alternative paths are possible. We feel that it is preferable to refer to types of organization form rather than to stages. The multi-divisional form need not be Stage III. It can be Stage II for some firms who adopt a holding company form for Stage III. Thus the model proposed here allows alternative paths, permitting organizations to stop at any type and even to reverse direction. The primary point of the discussion is to separate what has been observed in a biased sample from what is possible.

A second feature of the model is that it does identify some stages of development. Not all paths are possible. An organization cannot move to a global form without passing through a domestic type as well. A simple organization cannot become a global multi-divisional without passing through at least one transitional form. That is, an organization must learn to manage one and two sources of diversity before handling a third. In this sense we can speak of stages, but we cannot equate any of the types of structure, after the simple structure, with a particular stage.

TYPES OF ORGANIZATION

The previous section emphasized different types of organization, each of which constitute a different way of life. In this section we want to present our model of these different types. In so doing we will build upon the Scott model which was presented earlier. Our model is shown in Table 8.1. Its characteristics are similar both to those of the research we reviewed and to those used by Scott.

The characteristics start with the strategy classification that has been used throughout this book. They represent the increasing diversity absorbed and managed by large enterprises. The second characteristic shows the degree of integration between divisions. This characteristic varies from the tight interdependence between divisions in the vertically integrated firm, through the loose coupling of the multi-divisional firm exploiting some type of relatedness, to the almost self-contained holding company divisions. The structures that administer these relations are the functional, the holding company, and the multi-divisional (domestic and global) forms. These follow from the research previously discussed.

The research and development function is increasingly institutionalized as one moves from the simple form of organization to the multi-

Table 8.1 Model Illustrating Five Organizational Types

TYPE / CHARACTERISTIC	(S) Simple	(F) Functional	(H) Holding	(M) Multi-Divisional	(G) Global—(M)
Strategy	Single Product	Single Product and Vertical integration	Growth by Acquisition unrelated diversity	Related diversity of product lines—internal growth some acquisition	Multiple products in multiple countries
Inter-unit and Market Relations					
Organization Structure	Simple functional	Central functional	Decentralized Profit Centers around product divisions Small Headquarters	Decentralized Product or area division profit centers	Decentralized profit centers around World wide product or area divisions
Research and Development	Not institutionalized Random search	Increasingly institutionalized around product and process improvements	Institutionalized search for new products and improvements—Decentralized to divisions	Institutionalized search for new products and improvements—Centralized guidance	Institutionalized search for new products which is centralized and decentralized in centers of expertise
Performance Measurement	By personal contact subjective	Increasingly impersonal based on cost, productivity but still subjective	Impersonal based on return on investment and profitability	Impersonal, based on return on investment profitability with some subjective contribution to whole	Impersonal with multiple goals like ROI, profit tailored to product and country
Rewards	Unsystematic paternalistic based on loyalty	Increasingly related to performance around productivity and volume	Formula based bonus on ROI or profitability Equity rewards	Bonus based on profit performance but more subjective than holding—Cash rewards	Bonus based on multiple planned goals More discretion Cash rewards
Careers	Single function specialist	Functional specialists with some generalist interfunctional moves	Cross function but intra-divisional	Cross functional interdivisional and corporate-divisional moves	Interdivisional Intersubsidiary Subsidiary/Corporate moves
Leader Style and Control	Personal Control of strategic and operating decisions by top management	Top control of Strategic decisions Some delegation of operations three plans, procedures	Almost complete delegation of operations and strategy within existing businesses Indirect control three results and selection of management and capitol funding	Delegation of operations with indirect control three results Some decentralization of strategy within existing business	Delegation of operations with indirect control three results according to plan Some delegation of strategy within countries and existing businesses Some political delegation
Strategic Choices	Need of owner vs. needs of firm	Degree of integration Market share Breadth of Product line	Degree of diversity Types of business Acquisition targets Entry and Exit from businesses	Allocation of resources by business Exit and Entry from businesses Rate of Growth	Allocation of resources across businesses and countries Exit and entry into businesses and countries Degree of ownership and type of country Involvement

divisionals. The functional organizations orient their research and development toward improvements of product and process. The holding company and multi-divisional types institutionalize the search for new products. In the holding company, the search is completely decentralized. In the multidivisional, there is usually a centralized research and development function with product line extensions and process improvements decentralized to the divisions. The global multi-divisional is usually somewhere between the holding company (H) and the multi-divisional (M) form. Centers of expertise develop or are acquired in various countries. Thus, although some new product search is decentralized, it is coordinated centrally.

The measurement of performance becomes more formal and explicit as a firm progresses from the S form to the F form and then to the H and M forms. The H, M and G forms all explicitly measure performance against plan, but H form gives the clearest measures. The relatedness of the M form strategy and market, and political variations encountered by the G form all require multiple measures and some subjective assessments. Similarly, as a firm moves from the S form to others, the rewards are more systematically tied to performance. The H form again is the clearest, with formula based bonuses which most often take the form of equity compensation. The M and G forms also tie bonuses to performance, but use other indices and assessments for base salary.

Another major characteristic that changes is the career path followed by top management. In the S and F forms they are usually functional specialists, with a few generalists in the F form. The H form requires more general managers; therefore, one finds cross functional careers. However, they are predominantly intra-divisional careers. It is in the M form and particularly the G form that one finds the greatest need for general managers and general managers with international experience, respectively. Each type needs managers who have experienced multiple sources of diversity. This experience is the greatest difference between the G form and the others. It requires managers with interfunctional, interdivisional, and international experience: these renaissance people are part of the unifying substance that holds these far flung enterprises together.

The style of leadership and control changes significantly with the type of organization. In the S form, the leader is a decision maker very involved in strategy and operations. As a firm moves to F and M forms, the leader increasingly delegates operational decisions which are indirectly controlled through performance measures and procedures. In the M and G forms, some strategic decisions within the existing business are delegated to the divisions. The H form has the greatest amount of delegation and the greatest degree of indirect control through performance measures and rewards tied to performance.

The strategic choices are the same as the Scott model. The choices involved increasing choices about entry into and exit from various businesses, markets, and countries. For the G form, there is the choice of type of relation with a country. A firm can invest in its own facilities, use a joint venture, find a licensee, sign a management contract, and so on. Here the choice is the amount of risk to be managed.

The firm changes all these characteristics when moving from one form to another. Collectively the characteristics constitute the way of life of the organization. They form an integrated whole which fit together to permit effective implementation of the respective strategies. When the organization changes strategies, these characteristics must be disengaged, realigned, and reconnected. This change constitutes a metamorphosis.

SUMMARY

A number of the growth models have been reviewed in this chapter. All present a sequence of stages through which all organizations must pass. The models differ in the number of stages, but are similar in all other respects. They see the change from one stage to another as a metamorphosis leading to a qualitatively different structure. The reason is that each stage consists of a package of structures, processes, systems, rewards, managerial styles, and so on. A movement to a new stage is a repackaging of all dimensions.

The three-stage model proposed by Scott has been the most popular and is most used in the empirical studies, which support the three-stage models. However, when we consider international expansions, variations on the Stage III multi-divisional structure must be introduced. The variations in form also introduce variations in the paths, so that growth and development is not a lock step mechanical process. Organizations have a choice as to the path they want to take. The paths are not however, infinite; they vary according to chosen strategy. The chosen structure should fit the strategy, and vice versa.

A modified sequence of types and an elaboration of each type of structure was presented. An attempt was made to distinguish what is possible from what has been observed. When identifying types, one is led to ask whether or not we are experiencing a new type at present. Is the matrix a different type? This topic will be addressed in the next chapter.

9

Strategy and Structure—
State-of-the-Art

In the next two chapters we want to discuss the "state-of-the-art" in strategy and structure relations. We see two frontiers that need to be discussed under the heading of "state-of-the-art." The first concerns the new strategies and structures being pursued by the avant-garde companies. Is there a new type of structure emerging? The second concerns the scholarly state-of-the-art. Given this review of past research, where do we stand, and what do we know? What can we say about relationships of structure and strategy? In this chapter, we will examine the state-of-the-art in practice. The next chapter will examine the state-of-the-art in theory.

IS THIS STAGE IV?

The Stopford and Franko research is valuable in that they leave us with the question, What's next? They extended the Scott's Stage III organization into Stage III with an international division and Stage III global structures which we called the G form. The question now becomes, How much further can the global type be extended before it becomes another type? The question is specifically suggested in Stopford's diagram, which is reproduced in Figure 9.1.

What happens to worldwide product divisions as volume increases? Can they take a united stance to adapt to the European Community or Andean Pact regulations? Or, what happens to area divisions when they diversify and upgrade technology? The question marks in Figure 9.1 pose the question.

Figure 9.1 Stage IV Conditions

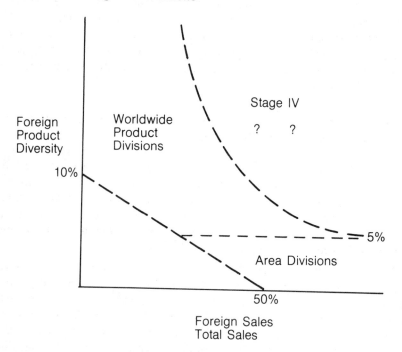

Foreign Sales
Total Sales

Some recently published work helps us to speculate about this question (Allen 1973, 1977; Lawrence and Davis 1978; Miles et al. 1978). The opinions of these authors assert that the question marks are being replaced by grid or matrix structures, and that matrix, grid, or simultaneous structures are indeed a new type of structure. Why? Because they represent a genuinely different way of life. We have always had multiple influence channels in line/staff organizations, but the matrix is an organization with two (or more) line structures, two accounting systems, two bases of rewards, two budgeting systems, and so forth. When the unity of command principle or the single tie breaker role disappears, the way of life changes. Lawrence and Davis describe the change as not simply a change to a matrix structure, but rather as the creation of matrix systems (budget information, rewards, performance appraisal, careers, and so on), the generation of matrix behavior, and finally, the institutionalization of a matrix culture. It is the matrix culture that is lasting, because structures and systems change as strategies and environments change. This matrix culture is essentially a conflict resolution system through which resources get allocated in the face of diverse demands for them.

If the matrix or grid is the new type of organization, then what is the new strategy that is creating the new administrative problems that are resolved by the matrix? If there is a new strategy, then the issue becomes one of identifying the organizations that are experiencing these problems and identifying the new structures that are being invented by them. These issues will be addressed in the next sections of this chapter.

WHAT ARE THE NEW STRATEGIES?

The central thesis of this book has been that choices of organizational structure and processes should be matched with choices of strategies and goals, in order to maintain the fit required for effectiveness. Therefore, if new structures are emerging, there must be new strategies and environmental problems that are causing a need for new structures. Such is the case.

The new strategies are those that add new sources of diversity, such as markets, to the standard functional, product, and geographic sources and give equal priority to two or more sources. The result is an increase in interdependence between product divisions, business groups, area divisions, or whatever labels are used to name units. It is becoming virtually impossible to find clean, self-contained clusters of divisions or groups that can form profit centers. For example, the firms in the computer and communications industries must cope with the coordination of multiple functions when producing multiple products, whose technology is changing rapidly, for multiple countries and for multiple industries. Thus, one finds product managers, industry managers, functional managers, and area managers who focus upon each source of diversity. But multiple sources of diversity are not the only problem. It is when product, geography, and market are of equal strategic importance that the difficulty arises. In the past, firms could manage diversity by choosing to organize differently at each level of the hierarchy. For example, in Figure 9.2 the electronics firm chose geography as the primary differentiating factor. Secondary emphasis is given to markets in an attempt to differentiate products going to consumers from products going to manufacturers. The next level differentiated between products. The product division was the basic profit center and was to coordinate the multiple functions, which were given fourth priority. The multiple sources of diversity were managed by the creation of multiple layers of management, each responsible for one of the sources. The level reflected the strategic priority.

Figure 9.2 Standard Divisionalized Firm Emphasizing Geography

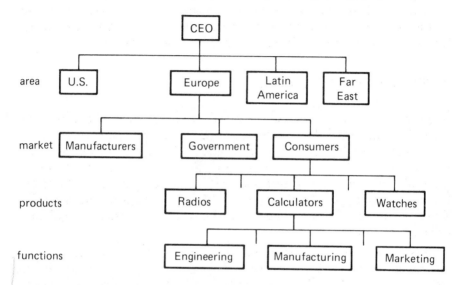

The problem now is that geography and product are of equal priority, with technology so important that a single large research and development function is needed. All areas should sell the same minicomputer system rather than duplicate the development effort to create their own. Also, the minicomputer system needs to be compatible with the large-scale computing system, so that they can be arranged to handle electronic funds transfer for the banking industry. The result is that some functions cannot be relegated to a fourth-level priority. Geography is important, but so are industry and product orientations. There is a great deal more interdependence across products, industries, areas, and functions. Self-contained profit centers are impossible to find, because there is a great deal of inter-unit coordination that needs to take place. There is a need for more general management to provide the coordination. This is the new administrative problem: How do you divide general management work so as to coordinate multiple and equal priority sources of diversity? Many companies are grappling with this problem and creating new processes for managing it.

NEW GENERAL MANAGEMENT STRUCTURES

The new strategies, which have increased the number of kinds of diversity and have assigned equal priority to two or more of them, have been implemented by many of the multi-national organizations. They have evolved several new structures for dividing the additional general management work that is needed when several sources of diversity must be handled simultaneously at the same level. Several of these solutions are variations on the hierarchical model. Others are matrix forms. The hierarchical forms will be discussed first.

OFFICE OF THE CHIEF EXECUTIVE

One solution to the general management problem is to add one or more general managers who create an "office of the chief executive." The number varies from two to five, and division responsibilities vary with the particular cast of characters. Some may be external, others internal; or, one may be international and one domestic. However, the key is that they think in terms of the corporation as a whole. Their performance is evaluated and their bonuses based on total corporate performance.

This form is chosen when there is no single piece of work that can be broken off and set up as a self-contained group. For example, international activity may be spread throughout all the groups and cannot be separated from domestic activity. An additional general manager can be added to be primarily but not exclusively responsible for international activities and their linkage with domestic ones. He or she would chair the world product line boards, in addition to representing the corporation in the executive committee, on the board, and so on. Thus, when the need for coordination is scattered throughout the organization, the additional management can be added at the top to see that the integration is in the best interests of the organization as a whole. There is also a need for a cast of managers who can work as a team.

A NEW SELF-CONTAINED CLUSTER

Some organizations are able to add managers and create a layer between the chief executive and the group managers. These organizations are able to find a cluster of groups whose work is interdependent amongst themselves and relatively independent of other groups. For example, GE recently added a sector manager who will manage all groups doing business in the consumer sector of the economy, as opposed to selling to industry or government. GE already has a four-person executive office and now has four levels of general management below it. The key for this choice is to be able to create a self-contained cluster of groups. When this option is not available, another one must be chosen.

GROUP EXECUTIVES WITH TWO HATS

An option that partially moves the organization toward a matrix form is to have group executives assume responsibility for two sources of diversity and, thereby, to wear two hats. For example, a geographically organized company had three major products that were sold across the geographic groups. In order to get economies of scale in product development, they wanted coordination across the groups. They felt they needed more than worldwide product boards. However, they also felt they did not need full-time product managers. As a result, three of the group area managers were each given a product responsibility in addition to the previous area responsibility.

The two-hat model is a partial matrix, because product managers in other areas report on a dotted line to an area group manager who has worldwide responsibility. It becomes important to manage the group executives as a team so that the inevitable conflicts can be raised in circumstances where they can be resolved with all geographic and product managers represented. Bonuses are usually paid on total profits, rather than on a product or geographic basis, in order to prevent biasing or suboptimization at corporate expense. The solution requires new processes and rewards in order to operate effectively.

The two-hat model divides corporate office work among the group executives. It creates an active management committee, instead of a new manager in the corporate office. In this model, group executives may spend up to half their time acting as part of the corporate office. This solution narrows the span of control of the group executive. Additional management must be added either immediately below the group executive or in the form of a new group executive. This particular form is popular among European firms. Royal Dutch Shell managers have both a functional and an area responsibility.

MATRIX OR GRID FORMS

The next alternative is to create a separate role for each source of diversity at the same level. This form was described earlier for Dow-

Corning, which has functional, business, and geographic managers all reporting to the office of the chief executive. Each source of diversity has its own champion, and the planning process is the resolver of conflict. Here, general management work is divided into pieces, with all pieces represented at the same level of the hierarchy. There is sufficient work for business managerial roles to be used, and businesses have equal priority with functions and areas. Care should be taken to recall all the processes, systems, and rewards that also accompany this structure.

NEW PLANNING ORGANIZATIONS—STRATEGIC BUSINESS UNITS

The last response to diversity that will be discussed here is the use of planning processes and a planning organization, which is different from the organization for execution. Many of these systems are labeled strategic business units after the GE organization. Essentially, these processes are program, planning, and budgeting systems (PPBS) applied to business firms.

A recent study by Allen shows that the adoption of sophisticated planning, reward, and evaluation systems are the latest organizational innovations being created and adopted by American enterprise (1976). Using a sample of forty American corporations, Allen followed changes in structure and process from 1970 to 1974. He found little change in structure but extensive changes in processes and systems. Many of these changes are probably attributable to the adoption of some form of the strategic business unit (SBU) structure. In order to explain this new structure, we will describe the OST system used at Texas Instruments. Then, other variations will be described.

THE OST SYSTEM AND TEXAS INSTRUMENTS

The Objectives, Strategies, and Tactics System (OST) at Texas Instruments is one of the oldest of the new generation of planning systems. It was started in 1962 and was felt to be fully operational in 1967. Until that time, TI operated as most U.S. enterprise did with the standard divisionalized structure shown in Figure 9.3. This structure was successful in generating TI's growth by decentralizing the short-run operations to Product/Customer Centers (PCCs). These units were $1 to $80 million businesses and were the basic profit centers. Long-range activity was concentrated in the top management, with the group and division managers serving as translators. In the

Figure 9.3 Texas Instrument's Divisionalized Structure

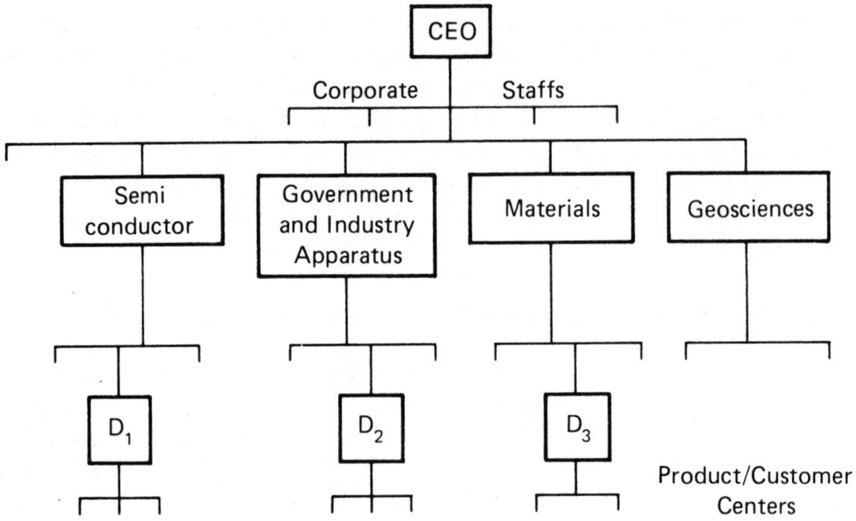

early 1960s, however, a shaking out of the semiconductor industry and the loss of some government contracts caused a reexamination of the TI structure and process.

Several problems were found. The PCCs tended to duplicate expensive specialist resources with little sharing. Each PCC was operating for its own benefit. Although this focused short-run thinking was a strength, it was also a liability. It generated small thinking in that new product ideas were keyed to existing capabilities or incremental expansions. There was no way to call upon the resources of the entire corporation when several PCCs were operating in Europe or in the same market. There was interdependence across the PCCs for many long-range programs. The OST system was created to tap this source of interdependence by focusing on the strategic long-range goals of the company.

The OST system was created to supplement, not replace, the PCC structure. In essence, the PCC structure remains as it is shown in Figure 9.3 and is the structure for the execution and achievement of this year's budget. The OST system is used for planning and resource allocation. The people are the same, however, and must handle a short-run operating responsibility and a long-run strategic responsibility. The next paragraphs will describe the OST structure and how it operates.

The OST structure, shown in Figure 9.4, is similar to the divisionalized structure. At the top is the overall corporate objective that is to be achieved by nine business objectives. The business objectives are relatively stable businesses in which TI will operate. They are chosen and defined by the top management and the corporate development function. Each is a fairly self-contained business, and the objective states its charter and sales, profit, ROI, and market penetration targets for a ten- to fifteen-year period. Objectives may be for the auto industry or for Europe. Quite often, they cut across the group and division structure shown in Figure 9.3.

Figure 9.4 The Texas Instrument OST Structure

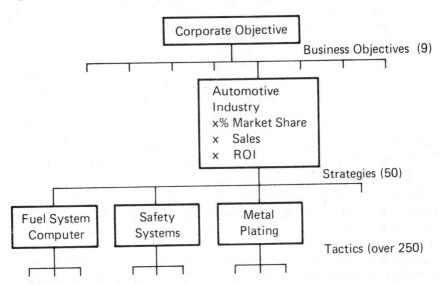

For each objective, there is an objective manager. The objective manager for the automotive objective might be the group executive for semiconductors, since most of the sales will come from that area. Therefore, that executive is responsible for the strategic direction and coordination of the automotive objective and, simultaneously, for the short-run profit performance of the semiconductor group. A rule of thumb would be that 20 percent of the manager's time is to be spent on OST work.

Each objective consists of several strategies. Strategies are also stated in terms of five- to ten-year goals, with a time dimension and milestones to measure accomplishments. For each strategy there is a strategy manager. For example, one strategy for the automotive objective is to provide microprocessor computers for fuel systems.

The strategy manager is the division manager (D_1 shown in Figure 9.3) in the semiconductor group. He reports to the group executive for both short-run profit performance and long-run strategic performance. Second and third strategies are to provide safety systems and metalplating products. These strategies are implemented and developed by strategy managers in groups other than the semiconductor group managed by the objective manager. The safety systems strategy is developed by a division manager (D_2) in the government and industrial apparatus group, and the metalplating strategy is developed by a division manager (D_3) in the materials group. These managers have one boss for operations, their group executive, and one for strategy, the objective manager. In 25 percent of the cases, there are cross-groups and cross-divisional objectives and strategies. The role of the objective manager is to identify strategies across the company and pull them together into a strategic plan for that objective. The strategy manager plays the same role for the next level in which there are tactics and tactic managers who report to the strategy managers.

Strategies consist of several tactics that are six- to eighteen-month check points and are assigned to a PCC. Progress against them is reported monthly. The first year in a tactical action plan becomes this year's budget. In this way, resource allocation is tied to strategic thinking and to execution organization. The planning and the doing are linked, since the same people operate in both modes.

One of the points that has been stressed in this book is that one cannot make a substantial change in structure without making compensating and reinforcing changes in processes, reward systems, and people. Such is the case at TI. A couple of problems are created by the OST system. One is the matrix organization that is created in the OST structure. Strategy managers have multiple bosses, and there is the potential for conflict. Second, the managers have simultaneous short-run and long-run responsibilities. The conventional wisdom has always said that one cannot mix short- and long-run responsibilities in the same role, as the short-run drives out the long-run. The changes in processes, rewards, and people are aimed at solving those problems.

The planning process itself is designed to channel conflict into the planning activity where it is resolved. The strategy managers then operate against a single set of agreed upon numbers. The process starts with some 400 managers meeting for a week in March. At the meeting, each objective is presented by the objective manager and selected strategy managers. Guidelines for objectives come from the objectives and policy committee of the board of directors. This committee meets three times per year for two days to establish overall direction. Then, final approval of the objectives is negotiated with the corporate development committee, which consists of the top operating managers; the directors of corporate development, marketing, and research and development; and the patent attorney. This committee meets for one day about twice each month to review the OST system. The objectives are negotiated by objective managers after the annual planning conference. After final approval, the objective is reviewed throughout the year by the objective manager. Implementation falls to the strategy managers, and tactics are reviewed monthly. In this way, the budget for growth goals is allocated and managed. The budget for current operations, on the other hand, goes through the PCC system. The two budgets are integrated at the top through the operating committee, which consists only of group executives, corporate staff executives, and the office of the chief executive. It is in these forums with interlocking memberships that conflicts are raised and worked through.

Control over the strategic milestone is as extensive as that over the short-run operations. There is an OST information and reporting system as well as a PCC system. Tactic managers are responsible for over-and underspending on OST milestones. Both the short- and long-run are integrated into an operating statement.

—Revenue
—Operating expense
—Operating profit
—Strategic expense
—Organization profit

Managers are held jointly accountable and are rewarded for short- and long-run performance goals. The strategic goals are kept visible and measured along with the short-run goals. Both short- and long-run perspectives are part of the reward system. Thus, the information system and the reward system reinforce the OST system.

Another supporting process is the career movement of managers. Some attempt is made to have managers experience a line responsibility, then a staff job, then a line job, a staff job, and so on. In this way, the manager is exposed first to a task in which he or she must meet short-run operating numbers and exercise direct authority over subordinates. Then, the manager experiences an ambiguous staff job with longer-run responsibilities, in which, to implement policies, the cooperation of those who do not work directly for the manager must be secured. Those that are successful will be able to operate simultaneously in the line, in the short-run PCC structures, and in the long-range, matrix OST system. By this process, people are prepared for dual roles.

Thus, TI has created a resource allocation process to develop products for diverse businesses and markets. They have another structure, the PCC, for managing diverse products and technologies. The same managers operate in both modes. Resources are allocated through the OST system. Then, once the numbers are agreed upon, the managers shift to an operating mode in the PCC structure. They have one organization for planning and one for operations. There are reinforcing planning meetings, information systems, reward systems, and career movements that complete the fit between strategy, structure, and process. The general management work for strategically managing multiple sources of diversity is shared throughout the hierarchy.

Other variations are being adopted by other companies. GE adopted a Strategic Business Unit (SBU) structure in 1968 (*Business Week* 1972). The number varies, but GE operates approximately forty-five SBUs, which are similar to strategies at TI. The SBU structure is for planning, and the standard multi-divisional structure is for control and operations. At the moment, four SBUs are managed by group executives, twenty by division managers, and nineteen by department managers (equivalent to a PCC manager at TI). The level is dictated by whether the SBU is cross-departmental or cross-divisional and by the size of the business.

An SBU is subject to definition by a top management group that must continually define the SBU's boundaries. An SBU is to be a relatively independent business mission (i. e., independent of other SBUs) with a clearly defined set of competitors and the capacity to measure profit and loss. The criteria are fuzzy and require continual updating of the SBU's charter.

Other organizations define SBUs around markets. General Foods has a divisionalized structure that organizes different products produced by different technologies into divisions and groups. However, it has come to be recognized that the consumer thinks in terms of meals rather than products. He or she plans a main meal or breakfast and then purchases Birds Eye frozen foods, Good Seasons dressings, and Jello desserts. Therefore, some strategic coordination between the divisions on marketing and product development can lead to a more consistent offering. Therefore a breakfast SBU, main meal SBU, and so forth, were created for this strategic direction. In this case, however, the organization created a separate role of SBU manager, instead of using the existing line organization managers. Each SBU manager has a market development manager and a controller reporting to him or her. The purpose is to guide long-run product development by market and to achieve cross-divisional coordination. Once the planning is accomplished, however, execution falls to the divisional structure. The technologies for manufacturing and distributing frozen foods are quite different from those for puddings and salad dressings. Divisions should be organized for production on a product basis; only the market positioning and product development require cross-division planning coordination.

These brief examples are representative of the various SBU structures that are evolving to handle business, market, or geographic diversity that is being experienced primarily by the product divisionalized companies. The separate organizations for planning and execution enable them to respond to multiple sources of diversity and cross-divisional interdependencies. As such, these planning organizations are the newest source of organizational innovation, the new type structures that some authors claim them to be. The reason is the extensive, power sharing, conflict resolving mechanisms that are created, as well as the new information systems, reward systems, and career movements that go with the innovation. In the next section we complete the characteristics for this new type of structure.

THE MATRIX ORGANIZATION FORM

In this section the characteristics of the matrix type structure are specified and are added to those of the previously mentioned simple, functional, holding, multi-divisional and global types. Table 9.5 lists the characteristics of this new type of organization.

The strategy pursued by this type is one of multiple sources of diversity with two or more sources having equal priority. At Citibank it is geographical areas and businesses such as investment banking, corporate banking, and so on. The interdivisional relations involve some resource sharing, geography sharing, and market sharing. With the exception of the vertically integrated unit, this form represents the most extensive linkage between divisions. The decentralization and interdivisional linkage is managed through the matrix organization structure with its team processes and joint responsibility.

The research and development is institutionalized as in the M and G forms, but is managed more long-range through the SBU systems. One of the key areas of difference is in performance measurement. In the matrix form there is multi-dimensional profit reporting by area, product, and business. As in the Texas Instrument OST system, measures are both long- and short-range oriented. Substantial effort goes into the development of these systems. Rewards are similarly

Table 9.5 Characteristics of the Matrix Form

Characteristics	Matrix Form
Strategy	Multiple functions, products or markets or geography with two or more of equal priority.
Inter-unit and Market Relations	
Organization Structure	Decentralized with area and product (or market) profit centers or functional cost centers and product profit centers.
Research and Development	Institutionalized with central direction of centralized lab and centers of expertise performing work. Increasingly long range oriented to support SBU's.
Performance Measurement	Multi-dimensional with extensive profit, ROI and cost reporting by area, product, business and function for short and long range.

[B7037]

different. Increasingly, bonuses given to the team of top executives are based upon total corporate profitability. Individual rewards are discretionary and based upon individual performance and contribution to the team. These individual rewards take the form of increases to base salary.

One of the biggest changes is in the career structure. The successful matrix requires renaissance people who know the various sources of diversity. Therefore multi-functional, multi-business, and multi-country careers are evolving. These people learn how to learn and to master the multiple languages associated with the diverse businesses, functions, and areas. A concomitant of this development is a strong human resources department to aid in this development process.

The strategic choices are as before. There is entry into and exit from markets, businesses, and areas. But now there is the establishment of priority setting across dimensions. Is a market orientation more important than product orientation? There is also the power balancing between the multiple dimensions.

The most extensive change that accompanies the adoption of the matrix form is in the role of the chief executive or office of the chief executive. These changes will now be described in detail.

The first role change is from a delegator, required by H and M forms, to a joint delegator. For example in a geographic/product matrix, there is a reporting of profit by area and by product as shown in Figure 9.5. That means that area manager B and product manager 2 are jointly accountable for product two's profit in country B. They both take the bows when performance is good and are both called on the carpet when performance is poor. No finger pointing by one at the other is permitted. This change requires a change of attitude from one person being responsible. The joint responsibility of the matrix must emanate from the top.

Figure 9.5 Matrix of Dual Reporting Relationships

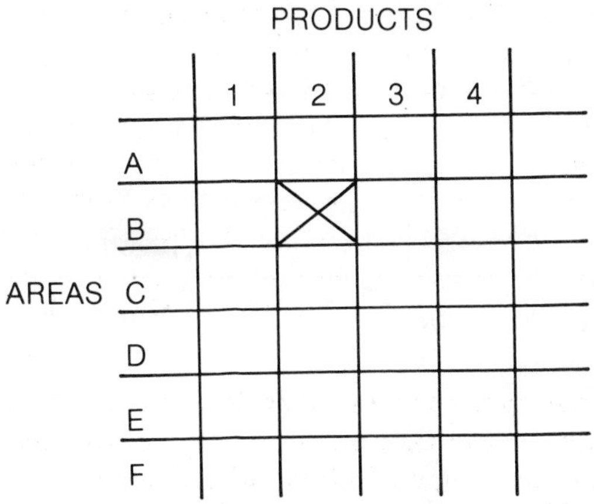

PRODUCTS

AREAS

The second change is management of the top group as a team. It must meet as a team and consider itself a team, and it may even be located physically together. This change means no more one-on-one deals that could be made in the H form and to some extent in the M form. As team leader, the CEO must initiate the team building and team management process.

The third feature is the increasing need for priority judgments. A characteristic of the matrix is shared resources. When two or more product lines compete for a scarce and shared resource, a priority decision is required. The chief executive should act as priority setter or manage the top team in setting priorities. If not, the priorities will be set on the basis of the "squeaky wheel," through back door deals, old school ties, or by lower level people who lack a strategic perspective. Any time there are more demands than resources, priorities will be set. The only choice lies in how they will be set. We prefer that the top group be the priority setter.

The fourth point follows from the third. The chief executive increasingly plays the role of conflict resolver or tie breaker. Conflict is built into the matrix by the presence of champions for products, for functions, and for areas. These managers agree to disagree and channel their points of view into a planning process in which the CEO resolves the differences, so that lower level personnel work against a single set of numbers and performance expectations. The inherent conflict is encouraged, surfaced, and channeled into a planning process for resolution. This means that there are lots of people going to lots of meetings. The linkages must be managed. Thus there is a premium on effective conflict resolving skills in the matrix leader.

Finally, it is in these conflict resolving meetings that the CEO acts as a power balancer. If the product managers are younger and weaker, it is in the conflict resolution meetings that the CEO protects them from the older, more experienced country managers or functional executives. In this way, the power distribution across the various dimentions stays in tune with the requirements of strategy and environment. The CEO increasingly becomes the orchestrater of a decision making process rather than a decision maker. A person can make only a finite number of decisions. But by managing the decision context, the executive can have an impact upon thousands of decisions. This is the major role change for the chief executive.

SUMMARY

In this chapter we have tried to present the current response to increased diversity and to the equal priorities given to two or more sources of diversity. These new strategies have created a need for more general management. This additional general management has been added in a number of ways, for instance, by a change in the office of the chief executive and the addition of a new layer between the CEO and the group executive.   Other responses exist by which multiple sources of diversity are handled within the normal hierarchy of authority.   The two-hat model is a solution that moves part way to a matrix form.   The matrix and the SBU models are new models requiring modifications in information systems, reward systems, careers, management development, and so on.   These new structures constitute a new way of life in the modern corporation and are hypothesized to be the new type of organization form.   The SBU model is a genuinely new form in that there is an organizational structure for planning and one for execution.   Members of the organization require the flexibility to move from one form to another.

10

The Strategy—Structure Relation

This chapter will give an overview of the state-of-the-art with regard to the research on strategy and structure that has been reviewed and discussed in the previous chapter. Specifically, what can we say we have learned since Chandler first put forth his thesis around 1960? What do we know about the theory that ties strategy and structure together? The last chapter reviewed the state-of-the-art in practice. This one will examine the theoretical and empirical state-of-the-art.

OVERVIEW OF RESEARCH

Many studies have been reviewed and cited throughout this book. In this chapter we will concentrate, however, only on the main thesis of strategy and overall structure.

The thesis that structure follows strategy receives substantial support. Large American and European manufacturing and service enterprises are diversifying products and markets. When they do, they adopt the multi-divisional structure. The relation is shown in numerous studies. Clearly, something is at work here, but whether the relation is the one suggested by Chandler is not clear. The research has created other interpretations and additional variables that moderate the strategy-structure relation. We will follow the Scott and Chandler stages model here. There is no loss of general applicability as a result of substituting type for stage.

Chandler suggested that the Stage I structure was invented to solve the problems of the Stage I strategy (volume expansion). The Stage II structure was invented when Stage I structures could not manage the Stage II strategies, and so on. Thus, effective performance is achieved only when Stage N strategy is matched with Stage N structure. When management adopts an $N + 1$ strategy, there is a decline in performance that provokes the shift to the $N + 1$ structure, which then increases performance. This sequence depicts the events at Du Pont that were described by Chandler. The observed lags in changes to multi-divisional forms following diversification also fit the interpretation. Thus, a mismatch in strategy and structure causes a decline in performance that is restored when a match is finally achieved.

The direct tests of this hypothesis have not been conclusive and are subject to alternative explanations. Rumelt ran into difficulty because he could not always find mismatches in sufficient numbers to permit statistical tests. This fact could be taken as data that natural selection is at work, forcing mismatches into matches. But the fact may be attributed to other factors, such as imitation of other organizations. In addition, the mismatches, although few in number, are sometimes the high performers. This observation is usually explained by the firm's having a temporary monopoly due to a hot, new product. When combined with the European research, these observations lead to the introduction of competition as a moderating variable in the strategy-structure relation.

The proposition becomes: Only under competitive conditions does a mismatch between strategy and structure lead to ineffective performance. If a firm has power over its environment so that it can control prices because of monopoly position, tariffs, or close ties to government, it can maintain effective economic performance even if there is a mismatch between strategy and structure. It does not have to engage in the difficult task of restructuring to bring about efficient internal resource allocations.

A couple of scenarios for firms under noncompetitive conditions are possible to augment the scenario put forth by Chandler and illustrated by the Du Pont case. One is that the adoption of an $N + 1$ strategy does not lead to a decline in performance at all. Thus, there is no motive for structural change. Second, there may be a decline in performance that is restored not by restructuring, but by influencing relevant actors in the environment. Thus, the relation is not always a simple sequential process of change of strategy, decline in performance, restructuring, and restoration of performance. The relation becomes instead a complicated interplay between strategy, structure, performance, and competitiveness of markets.

The second scenario raises another possible sequence of events. Under competitive conditions, an $N+1$ strategy and a Stage N structure will lead to a decline in performance. The interesting question is, What is the response of the organization to the information about performance? Presumably, performance can be restored either through restructuring or by influencing relevant actors in the environment. A third alternative is to return to the Stage N strategy and abandon the unfamiliar Stage $N+1$. Conceivably, this third alternative may also restore performance.

The three possible scenarios, which could follow from a performance decline due to a mismatch, introduce another relevant variable—the power distribution among the top managers. Undoubtedly, proponents for all three alternatives can be found inside the firm. The functional vice-presidents will favor a return to the dominant business, whereas the younger managers with cross-functional experience and MBAs will favor reorganization to the multi-divisional form. Both positions are self-serving. In the absence of a clear-cut solution, the chosen alternative is the result of political processes. The greater the ambiguity, the greater the influence of politics in determining the outcome and the greater the influence of the current distribution of power. Thus, structure will influence strategy. It is also for this reason that a change in the chief executive is often needed to bring about the change in strategy and structure. The current organization has institutionalized the previous strategy, and role occupants stand to lose status and power by adopting a new strategy and, therefore, a new structure.

Thus, the complete explanation of the relation between strategy and structure must consider a number of other factors. Figure 10.1 introduces these factors and illustrates some likely scenarios that can follow each condition. An adequate understanding requires knowledge of market conditions, performance, and the relative power of the dominant managers. An historical perspective upon the individual firm is required in order to untangle the interplay of these various factors.

The schematic shown in Figure 10.1 and the discussion in the paragraph above raise the issue of influence of structure upon strategy formulation. In the developmental sequence of strategy I, ⟶ structure I ⟶ strategy II ⟶ structure II ⟶ strategy III ⟶ structure III, Chandler focused upon every other arrow. One could just as

Figure 10.1 Schematic of Possible Strategy, Structure, and Performance Relations

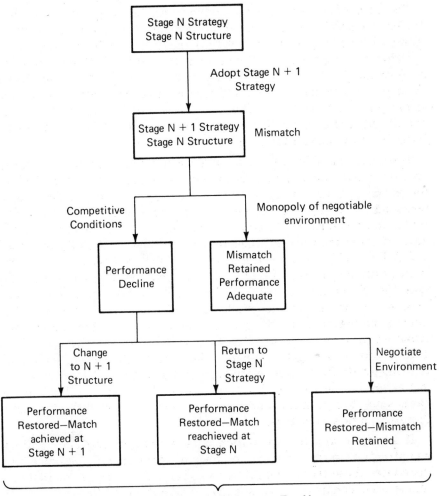

Result of Political Processes Among Top Managers

easily have focused upon the relation between Stage N structure and Stage $N+1$ strategy. Strategy can follow structure, also. Perhaps structure or organization can explain why some Stage II organizations adopted Stage III strategies, and some did not. If Stage II strategy is matched with Stage II structure, why change? Chandler suggests that changes are a response to the need to employ resources more profitably because of shifts and growth in population, changes in technology, and so on. But if you are already profitable, why do something unfamiliar? Some recent work by Miles and Snow (1978) begins to look at that question. They focus on the values and attitudes of the dominant management group. The management groups are then classified into types such as prospectors, adapters, defenders, and so on. The prospectors are managers who see environments as turbulent and act accordingly, thereby in part causing the turbulence that they see. Adapters are not the seekers of opportunity that prospectors are but will, as their name implies, change as they are forced to do so. They do not initiate, however. The defenders are those who stick to their dominant business and defend it. They see stability and arrange their environment so that it remains stable. How an organization reacts depends upon which of these groups holds the levers of power and what are the objective industry conditions. Successful organizations can be found among all groups. The important point here is that there must be consistency between strategy and all elements of the structure. It is not really important whether structure causes strategy, or vice versa, but whether they are eventually brought into line. There are many causal sequences in which change of strategy may precede change of structure. Or, performance may decline, precipatating first a strategy change and then a structure change. Or, structure may be changed first, in order to bring in new managers who will formulate the new strategy. There is no simple one-to-one relation.

SUMMARY

The point of this elaboration is to move us beyond a simple one-to-one relation such as structure follows strategy. Clearly, there are times when it does, but there are also times when it does not. Our purpose here was to identify a few factors that elaborate the relation without unduly complicating it, so that we can understand the choices available. Each factor (strategy, structure, and competition) has been shown to have its own independent effect upon performance. We wanted to identify when their combined effects were more important than each factor alone. The interaction of performance data and the power distribution among managers are the processes by which the alignment between the factors takes place.

Our position is, "It doesn't matter what you do, just so long as you do it well." That is, there are multiple solutions to any situation. What is important is to choose one of those solutions and pursue it. The firm should match its structure to its strategy, match all the components of the organization with one another and match the strategy with the environment. The challenge is to understand, to learn how to manage, and to learn how to talk about the power dynamics that take place in the determination of the chosen strategy and structure. When stakes are high, when dedicated people win and lose and some people are hurt, these are crucial choices. The choices require greater understanding from theoretical, practical and ethical perspectives.

REFERENCES

Aharoni, Yair. *The Foreign Investment Decision Process.* Boston: Division of Research, Harvard Business School, 1966.

Akerman, Robert W. "Influence of Integration and Diversity on the Investment Process." *Administrative Science Quarterly,* 15 (1970): 341–352.

Allen, Stephen A. "Fourth Generation Organizations: Problems, Emerging Sollutions and Human Implications," unpublished paper presented at IEEE Systems, Man and Cybernetics Conference, Boston, November, 1973.

———. "A Taxonomy of Organizational Choices in Divisionalized Companies," working paper, IMEDE, Lausanne, Switzerland, October, 1976.

Bain, Joe. *Industrial Organization.* New York: Wiley and Sons, 1958.

Berg, Norman A. "Strategic Planning in Conglomerate Companies." *Harvard Business Review* 43 (1965): 79–92.

———. "What's Different About Conglomerate Management?" *Harvard Business Review* 47 (1969): 112–120.

Blake, Robert R., and Jane Mouton. *The Managerial Grid.* New York: Gulf Publishing, 1964.

Blau, Peter, Cecilia M. Falbe, William McKinley and Phelps Tracy. "Technology and Organization in Manufacturing." *Administrative Science Quarterly* 21 (1976): 20–40.

Bower, Joseph. *The Resource Allocation Process.* Boston: Harvard Business School Division of Research, 1970.

Burns, Thomas, and G. M. Stalker. *The Management of Innovation.* London: Tavistock Publications, 1961.

Business Week "GE's New Strategy for Faster Growth," July 8, 1972.

Cable, John, and Peter Steer. "On the Industrial Organization and Profitability of Large U. K. Companies," unpublished Working Paper, Liverpool Polytechnic, February, 1977.

Campbell, J. P., M. D. Dunette, E. E. Lawler, and K. E. Weick. *Managerial Behavior, Performance and Effectiveness.* New York: McGraw-Hill, 1970.

Carter, Eugene. "The Behavioral Theory of the Firm and Top-Level Corporate Decision." *Administrative Science Quarterly* 16 (1971): 413–428.

Chandler, Alfred D. *Strategy and Structure.* Cambridge, Massachusetts: MIT Press, 1962.

Channon, Derek. *The Strategy and Structure of British Enterprise.* London: MacMillan and Co., 1973.

————. "Strategy, Structure and Performance in the British Service Industries," unpublished manuscript, 1977.

Child, John. "Organization Structure, Environment and Performance: The Role of Strategic Choice." *Sociology* 6 (1972): 1–22.

————. "Managerial and Organizational Factors Associated with Company Performance—Part I." *The Journal of Management Studies*, October 1974: 175–189.

————. "Managerial and Organizational Factors Associated with Company Performance—Part II A Contingency Analysis." *The Journal of Management Studies*, February 1975: 12–27.

————. *Organization: A Guide for Managers and Administrators.* New York: Harper and Row, 1977.

Child, John, and Alfred Keiser. "The Development of Organizations Over Time." in P. Nystrom and W. Starbuck, *The Handbook of Organization Design*, Vol. I, Amsterdam: Elsevier/North Holland, 1978.

Child, John, and Roger Mansfield. "Technology, Size and Organization Structure." *Sociology* 6 (1972): 369–393.

Corey, Raymond, and Steven Star. *Organization Strategy.* Boston: Division of Research, Harvard Business School, 1971.

Cyert, Richard, and James March. *The Behavioral Theory of the Firm.* Englewood Cliffs, New Jersey: Prentice-Hall, 1963.

Duncan, Robert. "Characteristics of Organizational Environments and Perceived Environmental Uncertainty." *Administrative Science Quarterly*, September 1972: 313–327.

Edstrom, Anders, and Jay Galbraith. "Transfer of Managers as a Coordination and Control Strategy in Multi-National Organizations." *Administrative Science Quarterly* 22 (1977): 248–263.

Fiedler, Fred. *A Theory of Leadership Effectiveness.* New York: McGraw-Hill, 1967.

Filley, Alan, Robert House, and Steven Kerr. *Managerial Process and Organizational Behavior.* Glenview, Illinois: Scott-Foresman, 1976.

Fouraker, L. E., and J. M. Stopford. "Organization Structure and Multinational Strategy." *Administrative Science Quarterly*, June 1968: 57–70.

Franko, Lawrence. "The Move Toward a Multi-Divisional Structure in European Organizations." *Administrative Science Quarterly* 19 (1974): 493–506.

————. *The European Multinationals.* Greenwich, Connecticut: Greylock Press, 1976.

Galbraith, Jay R. "Environmental and Technological Determinants of Organization Design." In Lawrence and Lorsch (eds.) *Studies in Organization Design*, Homewood, Illinois: R. D. Irwin, 1970, pp. 113–139.

————. "Matrix Organization Designs." *Business Horizons* 14 (1971): 29–40.

————. *Designing Complex Organizations.* Reading, Massachusetts: Addison-Wesley, 1973.

————. *Organization Design.* Reading, Massachusetts: Addison-Wesley, 1977.

Goggins, William. "How the Multi-Dimensional Structure Works at Dow-Corning." *Harvard Business Review* 52 (1974): 54–65.

Greiner, Larry. "Patterns of Organizational Change." *Harvard Business Review*, May-June 1967: 121–138.

Hage, J., and M. Aiken. "Routine Technology, Social Structure and Organizational Goals." *Administrative Science Quarterly* 14: 366–376.

Hall, Douglas T. *Careers in Organizations.* Santa Monica, California: Goodyear Publishing, 1976.

Hall, Richard. "Intraorganizational Structure Variation." *Administrative Science Quarterly* 7: 295–308.

Hickson, D., Derek Pugh, and Diana Pheysey. "Operations Technology and Organizational Structure." *Administrative Science Quarterly* 14: 378–397.

Hofer, Charles, and Dan Schendel. *Strategy Formulation: Analytical Concepts.* St. Paul: West Publishing, 1978.

Khandwalla, Pradip. "Mass Output Orientation of Operations Technology and Organization Structure." *Administrative Science Quarterly* 19 (1974): 74–97.

Kilman, Ralph, and Ian Mitroff. "On Organization Stories: An Approach to the Design and Analysis of Organizations Through Myths and Stories." in Kilman, Pondy and Slevin (eds.) *The Management of Organization Design*, Vol. I. Amsterdam: Elsevier/North Holland, 1976.

Lawler, Edward. *Pay and Organizational Effectiveness: A Psychological View.* New York: McGraw-Hill, 1971.

————. "Reward Systems," in Hackman and Suttle (eds.) *Improving Life at Work.* Santa Monica, California: Goodyear Publishing, 1977.

Lawrence, Paul, and Stanley Davis. *Matrix.* Reading, Massachusetts: Addison-Wesley, 1978.

Lawrence, Paul, and Jay Lorsch. *Organization and Environment.* Boston: Division of Research, Harvard Business School, 1967.

Leavitt, Harold. "Unhuman Organizations." *Harvard Business Review*, July-August 1962: 90–98.

————. "Applied Organizational Change in Industry," in James March (ed.) *The Handbook of Organizations.* Chicago: Rand-McNally, 1965.

Lorsch, Jay, and Stephen Allen. *Managing Diversity and Interdependence.* Boston: Division of Research, Harvard Business School, 1973.

Lorsch, Jay, and John Morse. *Organizations and Their Members.* New York: Harper and Row Publishers, 1974.

Mauriel, John, and Robert Anthony. "Misevaluation of Investment Center Performance." *Harvard Business Review* 44 (1966): 98–105.

McCaskey, Michael. "Tolerance for Ambiguity and the Perception of Environmental Uncertainty in Organization Design." in Kilman, Pondy, and Slevin (eds.) *The Management of Organization Design*, Vol. II. Amsterdam: Elsevier/North Holland, 1976.

MacMillan, Ian. *Strategy Formulation: Political Concepts.* St. Paul: West Publishing, 1978.

Miles, Raymond, and Charles Snow. *Environmental Strategy and Organization Structure.* New York: McGraw-Hill, 1978.

Meyer, H. "The Pay-for-Performance Dilemma." *Organization Dynamics,* Winter 1975: 39–50.

Mohr, L. B. "Organization Technology and Organization Structure." *Administrative Science Quarterly* 16 (1971): 444–459.

Morse, John, and Darroch Young. "Personality Development and Task Choices: A Systems View." *Human Relations* 26 (1973): 307–324.

Negandhi, Anant, and Bernard Reimann. "A Contingency Theory of Organization Re-examined in the Context of a Developing Country." *Academy of Management Journal* 15 (1972): 137–146.

————. "Organization Structure and Effectiveness: A Canonical Analysis." in Kilman, Pondy, and Slevin (eds.) *The Management of Organization Design*, Vol. II. Amsterdam: Elsevier/North Holland, 1976.

Pavan, Robert. "Strategy and Structure in Italian Enterprise." Unpublished Doctoral Dissertation, Harvard Business School, 1972.

Pennings, Johannes. "The Relevance of the Structural-Contingency Model for Organizational Effectiveness." *Administrative Science Quarterly* 20 (1975): 393–410.

Perrow, Charles. "A Framework for the Comparative Analysis of Organization." *American Sociological Review* 32 (1967): 195–208.

————. "The Bureaucratic Paradox: The Efficient Organization Centralizes in Order to Decentralize." *Organization Dynamics,* Spring 1977: 3–14.

Pfeffer, Jeffrey, and Huseyin Leblebici. "The Effect of Competition on Some Dimensions of Organizational Structure." *Social Forces* 52 (1973): 268–279.

Pitts, Robert A. "Incentive Compensation and Organization Design." *Personnel Journal* 53 (1974): 338–348.

————. "Strategies and Structures for Diversification," *Academy of Management Journal* 20 (1977): 197–208.

Poensgen, Otto. "Organizational Structure, Context and Performance." Working Paper No. 74–49, European Institute for Advanced Studies in Management, Nov. 1974.

Pooley-Dias, Gareth. "Strategy and Structure of French Enterprise." Unpublished Doctoral Dissertation, Harvard Business School, 1972.

Pugh, Derek, D. J. Hickson and C. R. Hinnings. "An Empirical Taxonomy of Structures of Work Organizations." *Administrative Science Quarterly* 14 (1969): 115–126.

Rumelt, Richard. *Strategy, Structure and Economic Performance.* Boston: Division of Research, Harvard Business School, 1974.

Salter, Malcolm. "Stages of Corporate Development." *Journal of Business Policy* 1 (1970): 40–57.

————. "Tailor Incentive Compensation to Strategy, *Harvard Business Review* 51 (1973): 94–102.

Scott, Bruce R. "Stages of Corporate Development," 9–371–294, BP 998, Intercollegiate Case Clearinghouse, Harvard Business School, 1971.

————. "The Industrial State: Old Myths and New Realities." *Harvard Business Review* 51 (1973): 133–148.

Simonetti, Jack, and F. Glenn Boseman. "The Impact of Market Competition on Organization Structure and Effectiveness: A Cross Cultural Study." *Academy of Management Journal* 18 (1975): 631–637.

Smith, William, and R. Charmoz. "Coordinate Line Management," Working Paper, Searle International, Chicago, Illinois, February 1975.

Starbuck, William. "Organizational Growth and Development," in J. G. March (ed.) *Handbook of Organization.* Chicago: Rand-McNally, 1965.

————. *Organizational Growth and Development.* London: Penguin Books, 1971.

Stopford, John. "Growth and Organizational Change in the Multi-National Field." Unpublished Doctoral Dissertation, Harvard Business School, 1968.

Stopford, John, and Louis Wells. *Managing the Multinational Enterprise.* London: Longmans, 1972.

Thanheiser, Heinz. "Strategy and Structure of German Firms." Unpubblished Doctoral Dissertation, Harvard Business School, 1972.

Thompson, James D. *Organizations in Action.* New York: McGraw-Hill, 1967.

Udy, Stanley. *Organization of Work.* New Haven, Connecticut: Human Resources Area Files Press, 1959.

Van de Ven, A. H., and A. C. Delbecq. "A Task Contingent Model of Work Unit Structure." *Administrative Science Quarterly*, June 1974: 183–197.

Van Maanen, John, and Edgar Schein. "Career Development," in Hackman and Suttle (eds.) *Improving Life at Work*. Santa Monica, California: Goodyear Press, 1977.

Williamson, Oliver. *Corporate Control and Business Behavior*. Englewood Cliffs, N. J.: Prentice Hall, 1970.

―――. *Markets and Hierarchies*. New York: The Free Press, 1975.

Woodward, Joan. *Industrial Organization: Theory and Practice*. London: Oxford University Press, 1965.

Wrigley, Leonard. "Divisional Autonomy and Diversification." Unpublished Doctoral Dissertation, Harvard Business School, 1970.

*

Index

151

†